FROM THE MOUTH

BY ERIK R. LEHMKUHLE

DORRANCE
PUBLISHING CO
EST. 1920
PITTSBURGH, PENNSYLVANIA 15238

Dorrance Publishing Co
585 Alpha Drive
Pittsburgh, PA 15238
Visit our website at *www.dorrancebookstore.com*

ISBN: 979-8-8868-3205-1
eISBN: 979-8-8868-3778-0

FROM THE MOUTH

SPECIAL THANKS

In the making of this book, my initial publication, I have several individuals that more than deserve my greatest thanks for their motivation to keep me moving forward. These individuals, I do consider true American Patriots fighting for the rights of all Americans.

First and foremost, our one true God deserves all due credit for this book. There were many times in the writing of this book where I did not know where to go, and among deep prayer, the Lord spoke to me and provided the light to keep going. Bless everyone on this planet and allow for every human the ability to sleep without fear for one night.

My father, Charles Lehmkuhle, is foremost my biggest influencer. I was raised a Republican but shifted more towards independent as my father showed me how to think on my own and not buy into what all media is selling. He taught me to think American and steer away from thinking political party.

My wife, Chantell Lehmkuhle, is the heart and soul of my being. I thank you from the bottom of my heart for giving me the drive to finish my book and see the dream of being a published author. It is my pleasure to have lived the "American Dream" with you, going from nothing to something. I'm very proud of you and love you with every ounce of my heart. Sorry for the hours and hours of domestic and world discussions that I'm sure annoyed you.

Pastor Clark Williman from Cavalry United Church in Van Wert, Ohio, played a large role as he entered my life in my darkest hour and, through the Lord, took me by the hand and brought me back to the light. Clark's compassion and hope for the good in people should be emulated by every American. Thank you from the bottom of my heart.

Everyone at Kriegel Holdings, Inc. in Van Wert and Piqua, Ohio, for taking me in when I had nowhere else to go. Brian Voisard and Matt Kriegel believed in me when no one else would and trusted in me and allowed me to grow in my profession to be the successful professional I view myself as today.

My loving children, Savannah, Nadia, Jaxzen, Zxavier, Brielle, Parker, and Grayson, along with my awesome grandchildren, Baylor and Charlotte, for the love and support even when I became lost in life. Living life is hard sometimes, and seeing how you all have grown from children into adults makes me feel very fortunate to have such great kids to brag about. I love you all.

My brother, Nick Lehmkuhle, I thank for the competitiveness, conflicts, and endless debates that we had during our childhood that developed into a bond that will never be broken. You are my best friend, and I'm very proud of the life you have built for yourself. Nicole and the kids have a great father to love.

The information patriots of Fox News that kept my American fire burning, Pete Hegseth, Sean Hannity, Greg Gutfeld, Laura Ingram, Tyrus, Joey Jones, Dan Bongino, and Lawrence Jones. If there are people out there that fully understand our rights as American people and how our government is contradicting our rights, it's these individuals. I may not be the ideal model citizen or ally, but I stand for your patriotism, just as I stand for our country and flag.

In Washington, I have a tough time seeing patriotic leadership that matches my passion; however, my list of patriots includes Ted Cruz, Chip Roy, Jim Jordan, Dan Crenshaw, and Lauren Boebert. These few fight the fight that I would fight, from lack of border control to Hunter Biden's laptop, I applaud you for your service to our country as you definitely speak my beliefs.

In the private sector, Mark Levin's fight for freedom is very honorable, while his book provided a trove of information that allows us to understand the history of socialism and how the Biden Administration is utilizing it to change our nation in the worst way. Candace Owens allowed me to see how one person can take on a nation against the odds. It is refreshing to see a young black woman expose the hypocrisy that occurs in our country when it comes to addressing the black population. She proves there is a better option and there are solutions that we need to consider.

Last, I want to thank all Americans from all political viewpoints that choose to come together to find real common ground. Strength in unity is the only way, while divided, we are conquered. Divided has never won a war.

Without the above-mentioned individuals, I would not have had the motivation or education to start and complete my thoughts with our national internal situation in this country. Thank you all and I spread much love to all of you as we are about to enter the heaviest phase of this battle.

PROLOGUE

The lack of morality of what the heartbeat of America is saying to the Biden Administration is the sole motivation for writing this book. I am an average Joe, American patriot. I love God and country above all, which for some reason will likely paint me as a white nationalist and evil against the Democrat agenda. This book is a left hook back at that tyrannist socialist movement. America needs a cleansing from these people that have a deep infiltration into our principles.

I am not taking a direct attack at the Democrat Party, as I fully understand that there are a lot of Democrats out there that are not in agreement with what the Biden Administration is trying to force on the American people. It is a fact that there are many Democrats out there that still feel the real needs of Americans all over the country but are silenced by socialist agendas. We must band together as Americans to cleans our government.

I do not identify as a Republican but rather a right-leaning Independent. I have no problem voting for a Democrat if that Democrat is attempting to move their constituents in the correct direction to individual prosperity, while allowing them to invoke their Constitutional Rights as an American Citizen. I do admit to voting for Donald

Trump twice for president. Do I think he is a PR nightmare? Yes. Do I agree with his policies internationally, economically, and domestic? Yes. Trump boldly went against the political norm and personally made me more money in my investments than any other president before him. Our economy experienced rapid growth, which will allow me to retire on time, maybe early. Under Biden, my investments average over a -10 percent loss. Biden has yet to address this issue as we keep bouncing around from extreme to extreme.

I spend a lot of time researching right- and left-wing media to see what angles everyone is trying to push. It tends to become confusing or drives people to radical passion. My position on it is everyone is at fault, and everyone is causing division. There is no moderation anymore, or level heads. You can't watch a hearing in Congress anymore without seeing and hearing some sort of lie or dodging of questions. This is unacceptable. Every employee of the US Government is responsible for answering questions in Congress. If you cannot, that is a sign as you are not doing your job the taxpayers are funding you and your department to do. Employees like Alejandro Mayorkas should be removed from government property immediately. I want transparency, I want to know the plan to exact specifics, and anything less is you not fulfilling your obligations to this country.

In this book I speak a lot about my way of conducting socialism. I absolutely do not agree with socialism in any form; however, millennials that go on to higher education and are indoctrinated by radical anti-alpha professors to lean in a Marxist direction need to realize that if it's socialism you want, there is a better way to do it that does have a quasi-successful structure. The structure Biden is trying to implement clearly models those of Castro, Chavez, and Marx. There's a better way.

My way is the better way, and if this administration takes away one word of the US Constitution, my socialist regime will be set in motion. Biden will be "Crushed by the fist of God." This country will not be oppressed at all. No race will be oppressed any further, no sexual orientation will oppress any further, no parent will be oppressed any further, nor will any child be punished for following their family morality against any political party objectives. Our at-risk communities will be fully funded with resources that will improve everyone's lives. Our education systems will be funded properly to improve our international ranking where we expect it to be. We will take back our control of international leadership without competition from China or NATO. We will fund law enforcement to be excellent ambassadors of their communities. There is a lot of work to be done, which my balanced system is capable of handling.

I watched a segment on Fox News in May of 2022 that highlighted Jack Brewer, a solid, God-fearing American that I am filled with pride while listening to him speak. Brewer advised the government to "draw the line" on several issues, but he mainly stressed the protesters in front of the Supreme Court Justices, which I feel is a form of domestic terrorism. The clear position of these people is to intimidate the Justices to reconsider their position on *Roe v. Wade*. What I understand from their ruling is that the Supreme Court is referring abortion rights back to the individual states. I don't understand what the protesters are complaining about. The states will get to create that law to reflect the majority of their constituents. This is what America stands for. Protesting this ruling is anti-American. Jack Brewer is correct in his rendition that a line needs to be drawn and being "lukewarm" will no longer work. Let's draw that line as to what is American according to what our nation was built on, God and country. Scratch "Build Back Better" and let's Bring Back the Pride.

I truly hope that this message reaches every American and we all can come together and reach common ground so this nation can move forward. Socialism will not work for us. I refuse to have my life restricted by a government that thinks they are above me and my people. Let's start a movement of love and positive advancement. I cannot do it alone. I expect 350 million Americans to follow my lead. The decision is yours, while I will not stop fighting for this nation.

CHAPTER 1
HISTORICAL SYNAPSE EVOLUTION

Since the beginning of mankind, our behavior has not changed all that much. We wake up every day and face some form of adversity, whether it is picking an outfit to wear to work or figuring out how to pay the next mortgage. In prehistoric times of the neanderthal, that behavior is still fact. They would arise with the sun and figure out what and how they were going to eat to survive until tomorrow. As humanity evolves, the one certainty that still exists will always be, *I have an obstacle in front of me and I'm going to have to exert some sort of energy to overcome that obstacle.*

Today, society faces much more complex issues that are more widespread due to advancements in social media and how quick we can obtain information almost in real time. With rapid information intake comes an overload of emotions without having time to process all the information obtained. For example, when Alexandria Ocasio-Cortez tweets that Ted Cruz is a hypocrite for complaining about the border wall being a national security problem, half the population will agree with the tweet and the other half with agreed with Ted Cruz. Almost no one will dig into the information to compile facts in order to see the whole picture as to what a proper solution should be. Average humans in society are preyed upon by our own government through our emotions.

The question all people of the world should be asking when obtaining information is, What is the problem and how do we solve it? The second set of questions should be, What is the intention of the issues at hand and who is saying them and why? The mind only acts with intention. When we wipe our nose, the intention is to clear mucus etc. Every single thought or action we have revolves around an intention. This especially applies to political social media and mass media. Everything from Fox News to CNN has an intention and most likely an agenda.

Both sides of the fence are responsible for starting fires. CNN gaslights racism, while Fox gaslights insurrection against socialism. Is this appropriate? Based on my sole opinion, I feel that it is not in the best interest of humanity to have so many fires burning at the same time. As extremely emotional beings, most of us are not capable of making sound decisions in a time of great crisis. This is also true as agendas that have been thought out years ahead of time surface at the time of opportunity. In the United States, we are merely tools of a governmental machine that has immense global power as to where we as working-class society are just ants in an ant farm. I do not find this as acceptable, as should you as a reader of this book.

What is the intention in highlighting racial tension? There are several theories at play here and we will go from the bottom to the top. Many ethnic groups are holding onto their American History from the birth of their settlement in this country. African Americans absolutely deserve their voices to be heard, as their initial heritage in the US consisted of cruelty within slavery.

The left wing of our government wants you to believe that there is a mass systematic racist society that we are all living in. However, it is a ploy. Systematic racism means there would be racism on a very large scale. In my eyes, it is difficult to see racism in our society. Yes, there are exceptions to every rule, but on the large scale that media and other extremist outlets concur, it is just not prevalent. Perhaps, though, I am just ignorant to what the majority is experiencing, maybe

I sit in a situation in life where I am not in the position to see such hatred. My own philosophy is to be kind to humans of every race and nationality or ethnic group in hopes that they will spread that same gesture to others. In order to have an unbiased view of what is happening, let's first define racism. Racism, according to Webster's Dictionary, states: "a belief that race is a fundamental determinant of human traits and capacities and that racial differences produce an inherent superiority of a particular race."

If this definition holds true, to stereotype average traits of one specific race condones everyone in that ethnic group to that same stereotype. For instance, an African American brain surgeon would be viewed the same as an African American drug dealer in accordance as to what mainstream media insists white Americans view all African Americans as. In vice versa, all white Americans are part of the Ku Klux Klan or Proud Boys, in today's expectancy. This stereotype may have been the public norm in the pre-1950s; however, as we have evolved and the United States Constitution's power to protect humans of all race and ethnic groups, this is not the case. What mainstream media does through the powers that be is to keep the wound open and dictate semi-factual information only viewed through one tunnel in order to initiate the end agenda. This agenda is preventative of healing and future progress. As we know, hate breeds hate.

According to BLM, mainstream media and whoever else runs with those groups, I am a racist, white privileged man that doesn't deserve to strive for anything else in society until the rest of the ethnic groups rise to my glory. This is the view that is being peddled to millions of vulnerable Americans across our country. According to the 2021 Census Bureau, 60.1 percent of all Americans are white, so 199,468,141 Americans are racist. Let's go ahead and subtract one from that list. I am white, but I am not racist. I have bi-racial daughter, have very close minority friends, worked for years with at-risk minority youth, employ and empower minorities, I could keep going on. It is also historical fact that at least two of my distant relatives served during the Civil War for the North, came to Atlanta, and helped burn the capital of the Confederacy to the ground as a distinctive statement of victory for the freedom of the slaves. I do not feel that I owe any minority or ethnic groups a penance or reparation. To my knowledge, no one in my family history ever owned a slave or treated a minority badly.

My direct ancestors immigrated to the US in the 1840's to New York City. According to family historians, once in the US, we were subjugated to intense labor jobs that the locals did not want to do, such as hard work industries like farming, cultivating by hand, etc. However, my great-great-grandfather eventually moved to rural Ohio, around the Dayton area, and then bought a farm around Lima, Ohio, in the 1850s. I come from a family of businesspeople and farmers. At any time have I ever heard of mistreatment of any minority in those records. It is my absolute refusal for anyone in my bloodline to be labeled a racist. The facts do not historically match the accusations by leftist.

What we all need to do as Americans are to stop and look around you and see what is really going on. Yes, Black Lives Matter started a movement to hold people accountable when bias occurs. They have that right and power, which we have recently found there are millions of misdirected funds by the organization. My theory does not revolve around a simple solution such as systematic racism. Racism is an easy target for higher powers to limit our rights as citizens. The left wants us to see things through a spyglass, when, in fact, if we saw our nation through a telescope, we would be able to come together as humanity of many races to stop the movement we are not seeing happening. My theory suggests, instead of systematic racism, we are indeed looking at more of a systematic mass oppression. This is not an attack based on race, it is an attack on the middle class, regardless of race or ethnic group. In socialism, you must eliminate the middle class in order to manipulate the mass. In the United States, you fit in three social economic categories, poverty, middle class, and wealthy. Most of our population fits in the middle class, which was created in mass from the boom of industrial manufacturing in the 1950s. This created hundreds of thousands of skilled jobs with a higher rate of pay. Many Americans found their skillset, and with that, the middle class was created, in my belief, for the better of our country.

When you look at what was intended from our Founding Fathers, they set up our country so the dreamers of that time could come to a new land with new leaders that accepted growth and potential prosperity for all. Now, the plan was not perfect. In those times they made decisions based on what they thought to be in the best interest of the new nation at that time. We now can look back and see where they were in err; however, they do not deserve to be cancelled, as I will cover more in depth in later chapters. This methodology was indeed set up to create a middle class. When we look at what our early European immigrants were escaping, they fled oppression from several crowned nations. For example, in England, you were either common or noble. There was no middle road. Once you were deemed common, it became virtually impossible to create a successful life for you and your family. In today's standards of the middle class, that has become unacceptable. We are still dreamers, always will. It is what our ancestors came here and today's immigrants still arriving here for. The middle class is relevant and should always be.

Looking through the telescope, is it systematic racism that we are seeing? In my research, it appears to be more of a piece of the socialist agenda, where a systematic mass oppression is the end goal. It is their way to oppress middle-class groups by way of guilt through creating a much larger racist exaggeration than what is really occurring. When you look on the side of the anti-racism movements that are going on such as BLM, what has the government done for you? Yes, you have power, yes, you have a legal movement that they unofficially co-sponsor, but have the circumstances really changed for the African American community? Did the Biden Administration dump a trillion dollars into your children's education, especially those in high-risk communities? In my opinion, if we are really going to make a differ-ence in that aspect, it is in the education process. Clean up the streets and dump money into at-risk school districts. In another chapter, we will delve in depth into our education systems. The point here being, the Biden Administration is keeping the African American community oppressed, just as they are oppressing the middle class. This is the ob-jective of progressive socialist democrats. Do not be tricked, my fellow Americans. It is a ploy that we can no longer fall for. Our American dreams are at stake here.

At large, are Americans systematically racist? I do not see that as what we are as Americans. Is that the fire that the socialist movement wants us to be in order to suppress the middle class's power? Yes, I believe so. In a time where wokeness clearly means sleeping, we need to really wake up and not steal away our history but use that history to fight for our dreams and success that socialism takes away from us. I promise you, American, we do not want to be stuck in poverty and treated like we are of a third-world country. Just research socialist so-cieties such as what Cuba is going through. This is the reality that they do not want us to see that is going to be heavily pushed onto our country in the next few years unless we stop it through our votes.

It is evident that there are several organizations and movements that are moonlighting as freedom fighters and rights activist, but in fact when you dissect these organizations down to their roots, there are a lot of communist, socialist, and Marxist footprints in play. The right is just as guilty as they tend to get overly aggressive when lead-ership is overly assertive. When we examine the January 6th insur-rection, yes, President Trump told protesters to peacefully be heard at the Capitol; however, with the amount of conspiracy that surrounds the 2020 elections, tensions were elevated, and the likelihood of a massive disaster was evident.

Is Donald Trump to blame for the riot that happened at the Cap-itol Building on January 6th? I don't believe he is directly. Based on ignorance and possibly lack of vision, he is responsible for the events that took place that day. Back in October, I viewed a video of the insurrection crowd on YouTube, and it appeared there was an older gentleman that was moving from group to group encouraging protesters to directly enter the Capitol building. The videographer of that film can be heard stating that older man was a federal agent planted to instigate the insurrection. As certain members of Congress had several days to prepare for the planned protest, it does make sense that federal agents would be among the crowd collecting plain clothes security while collecting intel.

If there were no federal employees among the crowd that day with plenty of time to come up with a solid security detail, there would be a clear derelict of duty on behalf of the heads of the DOD. It is absurd that we as Americans are led to believe that they did not see this coming and were not prepared with a solid plan to dissolve large crowds that become unruly. The greatest intelligence community on the planet did not do their job that day as either they were deliberately negligent or just plainly failed at their duty to protect all Americans.

Whether there was fraud committed during the 2020 presidential election will ever be fully known is likely irrelevant, but what is extremely consistent among conservatives and moderate democrats is that had our government been honest with the citizens for the last one hundred years, there would not have been an "insurrection." For example, I read an article written by Nathalie Baptiste from the *Huffington Post*, and as of the date I read the article, January 6th of 2022, she claims, "Trump incited the riot that left five people dead, and dozens of law enforcement officers injured. But while countless people are facing consequences for what they did that day, Trump still hasn't." This statement is highly premature and is exactly what is wrong with journalism and our trust in government. That exact excerpt, which Trump still has not been found guilty of inciting an insurrection, is a clear statement of opinion that is not backed up by any facts that have been proven in any court or congressional hearing. In our censorship society that we currently live in, Nathalie Baptiste should qualify for cancellation under liberal woke guidelines due to her lack of accuracy as a journalist, more so as an unqualified opinion piece

The only questionable information I have read about from the January 6th commission does support President Trump being neglectful for not coming to the forefront to dissolve the crowd as they broke through the first barrier enroute to the Capitol building. There are several witnesses and phone records that asked Trump to do something to stop the trespass of the nation's capital. As of the anniversary of the insurrection, there is no evidence that Trump made such effort to charge the Capitol building. In his speech leading up to the travesty, he in fact advised his followers to be peaceful. So, it does appear that, just like every other committee designed to discredit, charge, or impeach Donald Trump, nothing is going to come out of it other than wasted taxpayer money.

Looking at legal terms and federal law definitions are very important when making a public decision on who is right and who is wrong. After all, it is the federal courts that try these kinds of cases, not the media or public opinions. Federal law states, "organizing, promoting, encouraging, participating in a riot and urging others to riot" defines inciting a riot. Criminal code further states, "incitement is not the same as simply advocating ideas or expressing beliefs in speech or writings."

Under federal law and legal definitions, President Donald Trump did not incite a riot. His speech on January 6th at no time advised the massive number of followers to breach the Capitol Building, assault police, or steal documents and laptops of congressmen and women. It would not surprise me at all if the theory of a federal backed, staged, and manipulated insurrection were not planned out by high-ranking leftists. Democrats, after all, spent the entire four years Trump was in office trying to oust him. The Russian collusion ongoing investigation proved to be false information manifested by the Hillary Clinton campaign. They could not impeach him on the January 6th riot, nor will the January 6th commission turn up anything that can be viewed as illegal.

When you dissect the progressive game plan, democrats have control of the House, the Senate, and the White House. They can vote to eliminate the filibuster in the Senate to always pass their agendas through to Biden. However, their fear manifests itself vibrantly to me. If they felt confident they could get rid of Trump for good, whether it's a lifetime ban from public office or a felony indictment, they would destroy the filibuster in a second. I'm very confident that Pelosi and Schumer don't have a solid case to terminate Trump as a political threat to their agenda.

In early January of 2022, when Senate democrats probed their odds of passing voting laws by eliminating the filibuster, they found that they still in reality do not have majority support for President Biden. Senators Manchin and Sinema have both stood strong through the harassment and pressure from their own party. This is significant and will be noted throughout the course of history as the two senators that saved democracy.

As time goes by and we get closer to the November 2022 Mid-Term Elections, the Biden Administration will become more and more desperate as their policies and lack of honesty that Americans are tired of will be vanquished. It will be interesting to see if Biden continues down his path of self-destruction or change direction to better appease the temperaments of the American constituents. It does appear that Biden has a tough time dissecting the Quinnipiac poll that, in my opinion, is the most bipartisan and consistent poll that we have access to, which he is on a gradual decline in approval.

In April of 2022, Entrepreneur.com published an interview with filmmaker Ken Burns. I usually don't follow the opinions of documentary filmmakers; however, the headline triggered my inability to click on the article, which were headlined "Ken Burns: 'Mark Zuckerberg Should Be in Jail.'" I think it's fair to say that most conservatives would like to see the Facebook CEO in a dark, torturous prison somewhere in a faraway land. Burns agreed to the article to help promote his new documentary, "Benjamin Franklin and the Current State of our Nation," which I will be watching when it is released. I found one of Burns' statements captured me for a moment in thought, as it read, "In nature, a web is a trap. You get stuck in it, and then you get killed." In today's tech heavy society, we are all often caught in that web, and with it comes a massive amount of information from many different angles. In closing, Burns stated, "We're too static right now. Everything is frozen because of this interest in ourselves. We have become focused on the transactional, rather than the transformational." I find this excerpt to be very accurate in today's status of humans. We are just buying and selling, figuratively and metaphorically, when, in fact, nothing changes this way. If we see an issue in life, it would be a betterment in the progression of society if we take the time to transform the issues in a way that brings a bit of peace. Maybe that is too much to swallow for some of you; however, as alphas, it is our duty to set the boundary and right the wrongs. We are the balance makers.

Burns' interview is relevant to this chapter because, as humans, we fall into that same set of webs repeatedly. It is truly mind blowing how even America keeps trying to push failed agendas every few years. At no time has the leftist version of the socialist movement succeeded for any set of people in any corner of the earth. Yet, here we are again, pushing oppression and death to keep the 99 percent from succeeding while oligarchy rules. I have been sitting around for the last ten years waiting for leading political science gurus to highlight our repetitive behavior patterns that reveal the same result as before. All the intelligence in the world and they are still making mistakes from thousands of years ago.

In perhaps the oldest strategic warfare book known to man, *The Art of War* by Sun Tzu, is still one of my favorite reads. In almost any problem we may face, Sun Tzu has a solution that will most likely overcome the obstacle. For instance, Sun Tzu stated, "The supreme art of war is to subdue the enemy without fighting." It is amazing as to how that excerpt can be applied in so many ways in our modern society. In a way, it is a very socialist method to consider at times. The passage also underlines that strategic word play and movements can in fact create enough potential adversity that the enemy will likely cut their losses and retreat.

Another great example from Sun Tzu comes from the excerpt; "In the midst of chaos, there is also opportunity." I truly believe this is the method Democrats are utilizing, whether directly or indirectly, to slip their agenda in on their own citizens. As Sun Tzu ironically utilizes the word "chaos," it is noted that the "chaos theory," according to Britannica, "is the study of apparently random or unpredictable behavior in systems governed by deterministic laws." What this is stating in relation to events, which I believe were created or benefitted from Democrats, is when an event happens that may not directly affect one person as an individual but may affect another that in turn causes a reaction from that specific person who is reacting, catastrophic events can happen very quickly. While the catastrophe is occurring, an agenda is implemented by a third party that benefits only the third party, while parties one and two reap the repercussions of their actions. Sometimes, it can even be party three setting the event in motion for parties one and two to escalate. It is basically the same system as the Overton window, except in a more drastic and brutal way.

If history keeps repeating itself, we will never put humanity in place to positively evolve from where we have been stuck for the last seventy years. I do not feel that we were not mentally prepared for the rapid development of our technological advancements that we have seen in the last ten years. Therefore, we have grown out of control as Americans, placing ourselves in an endless vegetative catacomb where we can no longer differentiate from fantasy and reality. Currently, this is my utter opinion; however, I fear if we continue to ignore the lessons of the past, we will self-destruct as a nation, which makes my prophesy fact.

As far as our left-wing obsession with racism, this method needs to die now. I urge the black community to step away from the very people that have been acting as your handlers and step towards a real solution, a solution for everyone's happiness. Elect the leaders that will invest into your neighborhoods and into your children. Let us be educated beyond our wildest dreams in mass. This is how we break the cycle of ignorance. The black community can no longer be dragged through the political mud that every politician has done to you in past and recent memory. If anything, we need to pay attention to the pattern the left wing utilizes when it comes to black issues. They will show up and grandstand, and when it no longer fits their agenda, they disappear. Be aware of this manipulative neglect, find your real leaders that will invest into your emphasis.

History repeats itself because we allow it to. At no time does this need to continue. America will survive this dark period if we band together as Americans and not as individual sects of whatever the government wants to categorize us in the census. We are people of American blood if you're standing on our soil. Learn to enjoy and love the freedoms given to us by our Founding Fathers, stand in respect for our flag and all Americans that fall under that same flag. Unity among the common is bigger than any government could ever be.

CHAPTER 2

RELIGION

One topic that I feel is being put on the backburner of modern-day sociocultural issues is religion. Everyone knows the story of how our country was built based upon European religious persecution. The fact of the matter is that the Catholic Church became too powerful while Europeans were trying to evolve into the next stage of life. Many did not like the Catholic Church's stronghold on family values and their still-existing political agenda. For one, religion should have no agenda other than to be a good human being to yourself and others while finding your spiritual connection to the God of your choosing.

In my study of several local religious denominations, they all seem to say the same thing. When asked to clergy if the church is well and what the status of memberships are, most reply that membership is drastically down, and the coffers are struggling to pay the bills. They claim that people are just straying away from traditional religious beliefs and some perhaps choosing a more scientific approach to explain the creation of life. This is the excuse that I feel our leaders of all religious sects are using to justify doing nothing. Whether people are just straying away from religion over a period of time or get too consumed in fast-paced new society norms, leaders are not stepping up to bring us back to the spiritual center, which I believe is an intricate part of the moral and spiritual abandonment that we are experiencing today.

Growing up as a child and into adulthood in rural Ohio, religion was a huge part of my upbringing. My father was a Catholic, while my mother was raised Methodist. I grew up being confirmed as a Methodist and later into adulthood converted into Catholicism. In my marriage, my wife had a difficult time learning scripture as the semitraditional lecture that most churches preach, so we tried a non-denominational Christian church with a lot of modern music and dancing. There were moments where I enjoyed the theatrics; however, all the entertaining seemed to stem further into your wallet. Granted, the facilities were immaculate, and the production was that of a PBS show, but I just could not get past the feeling of being tricked. I did not feel like I was connecting to God but being preyed upon by very calculated corporate church elders to feed off my emotions for a percentage of my paycheck. I feel this method of "spreading the word" is wrong and we have grown farther from God's meaning.

Targeting religion as my enemy is not my intention; however, we must get better and do our part to save humanity from damnation and destruction. As Americans, we are seeing an aggressive socialist takeover. As most religious leaders abroad in countries where the socialist, Marxist, and communist dictators feed on the oppressed, you can attest to the horrors of this social system. It does not work. The problem that I am seeing, where America, the great and powerful OZ, has become an old washed-up man behind a curtain pretending to be great. It is time to rejuvenate our youth, reeducate the masses, and evolve to spread the love of God. Why is this not happening? The reason is because our country has become such peacemakers as smokescreens that we have forgotten how to be loving humans.

You can look at every major sect of Christianity and see the same ending. Where are our leaders during this time of judgement? As I stated before, I'm not here to make millions of enemies, but it is time to rise. No more hiding, no more scamming for megachurches. We need to act before the evils in this world consume us.

In fact, the Catholic Church has emasculated into a very powerful religious and political machine. With 1.3 billion members, it would appear there should be some sort of function regarding what is happening in the world. Has no one in the Vatican come up with any kind of idea, or are we only looking out for good Catholics that have very little issues but yet continue to pay the ten thousand dollars a year for private educations? As a loving Catholic, I beg of the pope to look at what the United States has become and intervene on behalf of all the Catholics, struggling and well off. When 16 percent of the world's population is Catholic, the church does have a sense of responsibility as to what happens worldwide. We need to own our part in figuring out the solutions. Where are you Cardinal Sean Patrick O'Malley? Your church needs you.

Not everyone in the Catholic Church is keeping a neutral tone. August 13th, 2021, I was running on the treadmill while watching Fox and Friends, when their normal high crime segment came on. Just as they always do, the network threw up all the higher crime rates in all the major cities. The statistics were a build up to the main segment about a local clergy that refused to allow crime in Boston rise amid the "defund the police" campaign that many politicians gaslighted for the last year. Reverend Eugene Rivers has spent nearly two decades with the Boston TenPoint Coalition, which he co-founded. His work became so effective that the National TenPoint Leadership Foundation named him co-chair. Rev. Rivers' approach is likely against any method the left would approve of. Going into at-risk communities and confronting the troubled youth in the streets are not exactly the safest strategies one could think of; however, Rivers placed his faith in the Lord and made an exponential difference in the city of Boston. If clergy of all denominations would take this method and apply it to their own neighborhoods, crime would decline.

The Jewish faith is just as at fault. With a war that has waged as long as recorded history, Judaism has survived the test of time. Of all the religions I will mention, the Jews should be front and center, speaking about their oppression and near annihilation of an entire ethnic group. Had Hitler lasted just a few more short years, there may not be enough of the Jewish faith to even talk about anymore. The greatest lesson learned from World War II, many people from many different faiths came together as humanity to rid a far more technologically advanced war machine from murdering Judaism from the history book.

Fast forward and we see the war between Israel and Palestine currently. This back and forth of innocent people of both sides of the dispute being slaughtered in crossfire needs to stop. Overall, the Jews are generally a peaceful group of people, with their devotion to their process of righteousness evident. Much can be said that the Palestinians are of that same ethic. Just as the Jewish faith, the Muslims are very dedicated and disciplined to their faith. In my eyes, I find it hard to believe that these God-fearing tribal people cannot find common ground. Peace and acceptance amongst each other are easily accomplishable if someone of power and standing shows the initiative to take that anti-prideful first step.

That step was thought to have happened when former President Donald Trump tasked his chief adviser, Jared Kushner, with creating a peace deal between Israel and the United Arab Emirates in August of 2020. This deal was a huge step in the right direction to start deescalating tense and violent relations between the two nations. This task had not been accomplished previously since the Oslo Accord of 1978 when a treaty between Israel and Palestine occurred. However, the treaty was short lived, and war ravaged the region shortly after. What has happened since, President Biden began downplaying the importance of the treaty since President Trump made the deal. Furthermore, the pressure from the progressive, socialist democrats demands President Biden retract helping Israel, one of our greatest allies, from being too friendly with the Jewish nation.

Any policy that is anti-peace is preposterous. Any religion that hates another religion is hypocritical. There is no place in this world for hate among any culture, race, ethnicity, sex, or religious denomination. One thing that any view of Christianity and Muslims should both agree on is the story of Sodom and Gomorrah. For those that do not know the story of the two cities, God gave several warnings to the people of Sodom and Gomorrah through Lot to stop sinful atrocities or be dealt with harshly. According to Wikipedia, God ended the two cities because of several factors: "Inhospitable behavior towards visitors, the act of sexual assault, murder, theft, adultery, idolatry, power abuses, and prideful and mocking behavior." Does this sound familiar? Our moral compass is so far off when considering justification for world issues, especially when relating to the United States, that is does not resonate as reality anymore. I feel like I'm watching a government conspiracy movie all the time. This is a problem.

How do we come together as a people under God? How do seek our own salvation in whatever way your religion deems appropriate if we leave the suffering and oppressed behind? I call upon leaders of all people of their faiths to unite in one commission to heal their differences. We as children of God, Allah, the twenty gods of Hindu, or the divine beings of Buddhism need to conference upon peace and goals of unity. All religions have one thing in common: love one another. We have lost sight of what it's like to love one another. To accomplish this, religious leaders need to understand that multi-billion-dollar corporations, which sometimes includes countries, make money off of war and conflict. In other words, expect a heavy push back from several organizations. Next, there must be an understanding that religious differences do not mean anything. The fact that religions have warred and killed each other for many centuries is noted and evident. We cannot change the past wrongs that we have endured on each other. As humans in the world today, we can only work to better tomorrow. Come together, my leaders, and bring love and healing back to humanity. Once leadership has established the common agenda of spreading peace and love to everyone, they need to be vocal amongst their specific masses and parishioners. We need to meet our makers knowing we did everything we could to reach our people to live their life as loving people. This message must be loud and clear. A show of force within the worldly congregations will place a huge dent in the anti-Sodom and Gomorrah direction many political leaders seem to want us to descend into.

In Chicago, there just so happens to be a bright beacon of hope that I can see from my home in Atlanta. Pastor Corey Brooks leads New Beginnings Church of Chicago masterfully. I have gone online and watched several of his sermons and feel that he truly is a direct vessel of God. With the Chicago crime rate completely out of control, Mayor Lori Lightfoot making no strides to improve the situation in the at-risk areas, Pastor Brooks has taken upon himself to make a significant difference. Pastor Brooks founded Project HOOD (Helping Others Obtain Destiny) to help fight back against the crime rate in Chicago, namely gang violence among the deepest crime riddled neighborhoods.

As many pastors across the US, Brooks opened New Beginnings Church of Chicago smack dab in the middle of the hood of Chicago in 2000. It takes an immense amount of courage to take on such a dangerous set of instructions God laid out before Pastor Brooks. I am sure as this calling came to him there would have been a small bit of doubt as to placing his church in the middle of hell on earth. However, Brooks bunkered down and allowed for the Grace of God to work his miracle.

Nearly a decade later, Brooks has one of the biggest up-and-coming churches in the country built on the trust and direction of God. Brooks also bought the run-down motel across the street from his congregation, which at the time was serving as a motel of criminal acts. After the sale, Brooks tore the motel down and is raising funds to create a twenty-three-million-dollar community center. His intention for the community center is to create a facility where education and skill can be obtained in order to get people off the streets and start their second chance at life as productive citizens rather than drug-toting gangsters or prostitutes.

Project HOOD is a huge initiative to help people on the streets obtain the correct job skills to work productively in a skilled trade. According to their website, projecthood.org, they have initiated a "Core and Carpentry Level I course, which places participants in entry-level construction jobs post-program, and entrepreneurship course, and separate business workshops for aspiring and new business owners, a co-working office space for business owners, job placement programs, and community-wide events including The World's Largest Baby Shower."

Pastor Brooks exemplifies what our leaders should be doing in every corner of this great country and everywhere in the middle. He exerts educating those that lack the skills to obtain skilled jobs that they can grow into solid careers. The community center will provide everyone in Chicago with opportunities to clean up their lives and learn to be positively successful in their own definition. Brooks' plans are bold and risky, but with trust in God and help from the United States community, I believe his system will have a lasting effect for decades to come.

I challenge other leaders of religion in our country to partner up with Pastor Brooks in order to spread his love for people of God and even those that are lost in their convictions. Reach out in order to make God one in organization, one in structure, and one in the battle against evil as it has its hands wrapped deeply around all of us sinners. Separate churches have a positive effect in a small community; however, a united mass church of all sects will intensify God's power and will against people like the guest writer for the *New York Times*, Shalom Auslander. In his Good Friday, April 15th, 2022, excerpt, "In this time of war and violence, of oppression and suffering, I propose we pass over something else: God, he began, before claiming God is hateful, full of Brutality, and, if mortal, would be dragged to the Hague." Auslander then went on to compare God's wrath to what Putin is doing to the Ukraine.

Leaders of God, your challenge is upon you. Evil can corrupt even the brightest minds. For the *New York Times* to publish such propaganda in order to cancel God is absurd. Auslander claims that God is too murderous for us to follow him. If not God, then who do you propose we follow? Joe Biden? Everywhere you look there is sin, which is why looking at Good Friday and the Passover is worth talking about every year. Jesus died as a human sacrifice for our sins. Jesus preached kindness among everyone from all walks of life. Jesus never killed anyone, nor did he ever harm anyone. He was peaceful and had no wrath. Mr. Auslander must also remember that God is not to blame for the sins of man. He gave us the will to choose. We do not have a predetermined destiny; we have choice to live Godly or not. We have the choice to repent and be one with God. In the Old Testament, when God destroys everything in a city, he does not choose who lives or dies, he takes everyone and sorts out who is worthy of the Kingdom and who needs to work on their soul purification. Auslander further states, "Egyptians young and old, innocent and guilty, suffered locusts and frogs, hail and darkness, beasts running wild and water becoming blood." Let me clarify, Heaven is a vast kingdom of greatness. There is no crime or hate. It is a much better realm than the hate-filled earth we all live in, so for God to take the innocent to a better place is an honor, not a punishment.

Auslander is too fixated on the small figments of our existence and not the bigger picture. I'm not an expert of the Jewish faith, so I will not speak on what I do not fully understand; however, the God I know and trust does not tell me to murder people or root for the killing of anyone. Instead of deflecting blame from free-willed creations of God that live in murderous sin over to God, we should go back and hold those in conflict accountable under law and allow God's wrath to judge. The point being that religion has lost its hold on love. Let's reach out and bring America back to our souls in order to set the standard every nation can follow as we used to.

When we look at the religious overtones of the Trump Administration, we can see why the Evangelicals believe Trump is the second coming of Persian King Cyrus, who were chosen by God to be king.

In Trump's four years in office, it is evident that the US was a much safer country than what we have been in recent memory. Many nations tested Trump, such as Kim Jong Un, dictator of the North Korean country/prison. Un launched several missiles early in the Trump regime; however, after a series of threats from Trump and a historical meeting between the two leaders, not one more missile was launched until Biden became president. World leaders feared God's chosen leader, as they firmly believed that if they rattled the cage too much, Trump would retaliate in such a force that would be catastrophic to any opposition.

Several countries also agreed on this prophesy as Israeli Prime Minister Benjamin Netanyahu, too, compared Trump to King Cyrus. In defense of this popular adaptation, Trump did promise to move the embassy to Jerusalem, as he acknowledged the city as the capital of Israel. When Trump fulfilled this promise, he also fulfilled biblical prophecy. In my religious studies, it appears that, according to the book of Revelations, when the Holy Land experiences their third era of peace, the Apocalypse will begin. Had the peace treaty in the Holy Land that Trump been put into play, it would have initiated a series of predicted events. My theory is that this land could have been set into peace over a hundred years ago, but religious leaders did not allow it to happen due to the start of Apocalyptic events. If Israel and Hamas are at war, we will be safe from Godly destruction.

Moving past biblical prophecy and simplifying religion, no matter what denomination everyone in the world is, except for the more devious denominations, they all preach spreading love to one another. This method is very successful, and if our leaders would reach out to people instead of parishioners, we would be seeing less crime and more love overall. When I see all the major issues facing our nation, I see children of God arguing, fighting, and killing other children of God. Are we that far from our religious roots that we do not see that hate does not solve a thing? Throwing insults from the left to the right and the right to the left, then seeing Muslims killing Christians and vice versa. This is just absurd and needs to be addressed world-wide. Our leaders need to come together and make a standout of love for all. If we cannot agree to share love to all, we will factually destroy ourselves. Go home and read your sacred manuscripts, no matter what you believe, and find where your prophets and divine historical characters preach love for all of mankind. If we as humans can grasp this concept again and develop a devout following to something or someone positive, this world will start to heal.

It comes down to what is holding world religious leaders back from making our world a better place. Let's revive our mosques, synagogues, temples, and churches. Leaders need to reach out to other leaders to create a network of love and support for all. With such a simple solution, it is a wonder as to why this has not happened in the past with success.

This is my challenge to all of those that wear the cloth and have taken that vow to the God of their liking. You don't need a church or money, you need ears, you need masses. With the amount of technology on this planet, it is not difficult to expand your message. Every single time I've gone to church in my life, I always leave feeling something inside me that burns for love. It burns for other people. As a church leader, you are more powerful than you portray yourself as, which is humble; however, the war is among us, and it is not the time to turn and do nothing. Church leaders possess the power that influenced so many nations for so many years, and now we are so broken up that the church has lost its way. Unite all faiths to work as one unite of peace. Buddha, Jesus, Mohammed, and any other icon of religious stature all portrayed their belief system in one way, through love. Love conquers all and we as humanity have forgotten how to love one another.

Must we never forget God is judging, and I firmly believe that God, although merciful, is also wrathful. If I had to choose which way he is feeling right now based on the global genocides and corruption, he will choose wrath as he did with Sodom and Gomorrah. When reading scripture as to how those two cities were behaving at the time God's hand came down in judgement, we can draw enough comparisons as to what is occurring today. Be ready for that same wrath. I feel we are near that judgement.

We also need to microscope religious leaders' comparison to the events that led to the Crucifixion of Jesus Christ. Why did the Romans convict and crucify him? His power for the word of God spread though out the Roman empire, which violated their laws. Jesus knew he would be found guilty and put to death and yet continued to teach anyone that would listen the ways of the Lord. In turn, Jesus was executed for teaching love with and through God.

Leaders of God, the task ahead of you is rigorous and full of doubters that will try to disgrace you and our Lord; however, if Jesus can die for that same belief, so can we. It's time to stop pointing fingers at injustice after the fact and move aggressively towards the love of humanity. We need to reach out and heal those that are broken. We need to draw heavily from the at-risk neighborhoods and anywhere else that could have a high percentage of evil lurking. There is a reason why the saying "God and country" have God listed first.

Clergy of any political leader in the world, you all should repent for your neglect of God's will. If your leader is not spreading love at all costs, then you are not getting the job done. There is a way to touch the heart of anyone; you just must dig deep into their souls and repair their hurt so they can love again. You will be risking your life in some parts of the world, but God's grace will shine bright on your soul at the next level. No amount of political litigation is going to heal this planet anymore. God's love will.

We must understand that even as our president claims to be a devout Catholic, he will succumb to the politics of his party, as he has allowed for Catholic churches to be defaced and invaded by protestors. In my lifetime, churches, synagogues, and mosques are to be sacred places of worship. There is no place in this world to attack those in worship and reflection. Our religious leaders need to prepare for evil invasions without the support of the United States president as he continues to show his true colors. Just as Trump could have done during the January 6th situation, Biden can do for the churches today as unrest over abortion heats up. Biden will even neglect the sacred state of our US Supreme Court. I firmly believe that he is a Catholic; however, evil has entered his heart and has pulled him far from his base. Catholic Dioceses need to be reaching out and reconnecting Biden to God and what God deems appropriate and acceptable. Instead of standing up for the Catholic Church and the attack abortion protesters conducted during sacred Mass, he ignored the complete violation that continues to occur on our nation's churches. Mr. President, you have the obligation to protect all Americans, even those that do not share your views, or former views, for that matter. Standing up for the church is not picking church as your Democrat colleagues want the left to think, it is standing up for peace. Get these God haters off God's temples, condemn their actions, and let's protect everyone.

It is time to tighten up our churches, solidify leadership, and unite all denominations against evil. There is a theory that the time of the fish has passed and the time of the taurus is among us. If that is true, religion is dead. It does not have to be that way. We can have a great reset. Let's purify our church, bring our leaders back to the structure God sets for us to follow. Jesus spread love throughout the Holy Land in order to allow for a massive wave of love, peace, and understanding among humanity during biblical times. Is there something wrong with loving one another? That is the base of Christianity, which has evolved into politics. Politics are not clean; there is no place for it in the church. Cleanse the church of all politics and move our faith back to its simplicity of love, nothing more and nothing less.

CHAPTER 3
AFGHANISTAN

August 15th, 2021, will forever be engrained in my head as a comparison to videos I've watched as a child about the conflict in Vietnam. Every news outlet seemed to show the same footage of a helo-evac. When you assess that day, it appears to look a lot like a spontaneous decision rather than strategic evacuation. Nearly a year after the disaster, Biden still declares the withdrawal of Afghanistan an American victory.

I have a tough time seeing this situation beyond what it is, a massive, spontaneous, impulsive, thoughtless maneuver that defied all logic. As we study this situation for the next century, as we do every major event in history, the intelligence community will likely be spared from blame. The US military have occupied most of Afghanistan for twenty years. When we look at policing in American, we know from talking to seasoned officers, they know where the trouble spots are and who the trouble suspects are. I feel that when you're in a country that long, much is the same. With all the technology available, along with the support of Afghan friendlies, I have all the confidence that our intelligence officers had all the data and information needed to conduct a very brisk, quiet, and professional extraction with very little to no American casualties. That is how good we are or are supposed to be.

When President Trump struck a deal with the Taliban, he successfully conducted an exit strategy from what appears to be what both political parties deemed correct for our country. As the deal concluded, there were not many on the left that publicly criticized our exit from the twenty-year conflict. It had to happen and should have in the Obama Administration. Under President Trump's plan, the US would have completely evacuated Afghan grounds by May 1st, 2021. Had Trump won the election of 2020, I believe our withdrawal would have been a lot less dramatic. In that agreement, it was well noted between Trump and Taliban leadership that if the Taliban conducted any further attacks against the US, "we are going to hit you harder than any country has ever been hit." From that timespan on, it appeared the Taliban took the president's threats seriously; however, President Biden has shown the world he is not capable of allowing the US to stand strong in the eyes of international policy.

As I am no expert military strategist, it does seem abundant in human nature of the behaviors and beliefs of the Taliban, added with an international observation of the results of a regime change, the Taliban just waited for their opportunity to retake the country in full capacity. The view of the enemies of the United States of America is this is a nation divided with weak leadership. Now is the time to advance our agendas. This is exactly what happened to cause the massive American embarrassment, which not only jeopardizes the lives of thousands of Americans in Afghanistan but also the peaceful Afghan people that only wished to live their lives free of violence and terror that we provided them for two decades.

President Biden also caused issue with several nations that also had boots on the ground in Afghanistan. According to Anadolu Agency, at the time of the rapid US withdrawal, there were troops represented by thirty-six nations in the NATO Resolute Support mission. My thoughts on this are for a presidential candidate to openly run his campaign on strong international policy, he clearly abandoned all consideration for anyone in the region, not only our own people left behind.

After August 15th, the president, along with leaders from NATO, began their PR clean up. The finger was easily pointed at the Afghan Government, while Europe and the US washed their hands and turned away from the twenty-year-dependent nation. By August 17th, the United Nations reported that the Taliban were going door to door to find all the Afghans that corroborated with NATO and the US. Women are also in dramatic fear as they, under new Afghan Government, were given new freedoms previous regimes would not permit. As soon as the Taliban took over the entire country, they exerted several propagated statements to the world media saying they welcomed the new women's rights; however, sources on the ground are saying they are in fact being forced to cover up once again and taken out of the social spotlight and back into oppression.

The problem lies in what the reasoning for the withdrawal are. According to President Biden, he clearly states that "the buck stops with me." Allowing for a humanitarian effort to extinguish because Biden doesn't want to deal with it is by far not a good reason to condemn thousands to death and severe oppression. Even under the Trump Administration, I understand that the president was sticking by his "American First" policy, which I agree on; however, abandoning human beings to the control of killers is not what we should be doing. America should continue to be the heartbeat of the world and uphold the compass for morality. Under Biden, we have never been so divided and lost, which now spills throughout the globe.

August 26th, I feel, turned the tide on the socialist regime in America. President Biden lost all credibility worldwide as a suicide bomb at Kabul's international airport killed thirteen US service members. As I highly agree, the prospect of death in conflicts are completely inevitable; however, when it comes to executing solid military movements, it should be minimal. There are several different ways to look at this debacle. My one question is, what were twelve Marines doing standing in relatively the same location? This seems like a problematic situation in regard to what their task was at the time. I would think, as a security detail for evacuation took place in a part of the world that is notorious for suicide bombings, you would not want to stand in large groups. Those soldiers were sitting ducks and easy targets. I ask that an inquiry be done to find out who strategically planned the extraction and secured the Kabul airport. This attack also killed almost 200 Afghan civilians that were trying to flee the country.

President Biden did give a half heartless response to the deadly bombing to which he is the sole perpetrator for this travesty. The fact of this traditionally unamerican extraction plan, it was not well thought out and our president failed to adhere to intelligence recommendations. We knew this would happen and nothing was done to prevent it. That is gross negligence on behalf of our executive administration and heads should be rolling.

On a positive note, mainstream media followed through and badgered our leader for answers and responsibility; however, in true coward form, Biden refused questions and routinely stormed off stage. After all, it was five days ago, who cares, right? Wrong! Act on behalf of our fallen like a normal leader with a powerful military. On August 29th, Biden approved a drone strike which killed several children. Now, the mainstream media did not give this strike much coverage, and I cannot recall one reporter asking the president to answer to the deaths of children. What changed? My theory rests in polls. Pollsters reflected that Biden is becoming overly unpopular, which in turn reflects poorly on the 2022 mid-term elections, which are closing in on campaign season. Democrat leaders in Congress started to backpedal from acknowledging anything happened in Kabul at all.

August 31st was the day that President Biden negotiated with Taliban terrorists for the US to leave Afghanistan. This date is the date that will live in US history as the day America lost the war in Afghanistan, along with our moral compass. In the meantime, our leader told the world that the US would not leave until every American was home. Later, his wordplay changed to "every American that wanted to leave." To what the evidence adds up to, if you can make it to the airport, you want to leave. If you can't make it to the airport, you obviously didn't want to leave. That's preposterous and genocidal on our leader"s part along with our military strategists. We do not leave our people behind, ever, period. President Biden later stated "this kind of thing happens all the time." No, it doesn't. If it has happened in our history, they were wrong too. Our citizens come home; our people come home. I cannot say that enough. The United States of America has the best trained, best equipped military in the world, so if we want our people to come home, through the powerful hand of God, they come home. There is nothing the Taliban or ISIS or anyone else in that region can do about it.

Stop negotiating with terrorists, Mr. President. America is the Alpha Dogs of this world. You need to act like it. Stop blaming President Trump for your second comings. Accept your own failures. Your poll numbers demand you take responsibility. With that said, the difference between Biden and Trump's withdrawal from Afghanistan are easy to diagnose. The world knows Biden is weak as a human being and leader. The Taliban absolutely understood Biden was in retreat quickly and many mistakes were going to happen. They also knew that there would be no retraction of the deal on America's end, hence the haste that we left with. The reason President Trump's withdrawal would have been successful versus the Biden Administration's is due to one reason, the world feared the wrath of Trump. He was a physical presence that the world saw as powerful. The Taliban all well knew that if they stepped out of line, Trump would rain fire on every one of them, just as he did ISIS. One factor of world politics that President Biden failed to acknowledge is the US apologizes to no one. We don't have to honor any deal, especially coming from a terrorist organization like the Taliban. President Trump accomplished this mentality masterfully, which is why one hundred million-plus Americans are die hard in support of him. This is where Biden fails as a leader on a world stage. He is singlehandedly responsible for the death of thirteen soldiers and over two hundred Afghan refugees. I feel the American death toll in Afghanistan is just beginning, as we still have many Americans trapped in that country.

As bad as Afghanistan turned out, we cannot go back in time to redo the mess Biden created. No matter how successful he states the operation is on MSNBC, Americans still died and many more left behind. We can still come out on top. This occurs by allowing out soldiers to do what they do best. Go into a country and get our people out. The administration should take heed of the true American Patriots, like the Pineapple Express, which is a group of former soldiers that have been searching through Kabul and bringing our people home. This is the exact definition of what it means to be an American. If Biden had half the grit these vets have, we would not be looking at dead American soldiers and citizens in a country we had full control over. If our administration will not save the rest of our people, I call on other American Patriots such as Erik Prince and Pineapple Express to do what our president doesn't have the guts to do. Save our people and those who want to live in a world where they must worry about being hung from our Apache helicopters. If we are truly leaving Afghanistan, go get our people and leave hellfire behind for the Taliban to never forget the day America left their wrath on the way out. The way Biden has abandoned his own citizens makes me think there's another story as to what happened with "cornpop" behind the barn. I highly doubt Biden got the best of that boy, as his leadership suggests he likely got popped in the mouth and ran home to his mommy.

When we look at the structure left in Afghanistan, we have to assess what we were going to leave behind as their government. Ashraf Ghani will forever be famous as the man who fled his country and stole millions of dollars the US entrusted him to utilize to make Afghanistan better. This tyrant had been president of Afghanistan for nearly seven years and should have had some kind of thermometer as to how to serve his constituents. But as fast as he fled his home nation, it clearly states to the Afghan people that he was nothing but a coward that depended on the United States to govern and protect his nation. As to what is proven with most elected officials, Ghani was an educator most of his career and had no military experience.

Going back in history to the Obama Administration, which was when Ghani became backed and empowered by the progressive movement, whom Ghani himself is admittedly a believer, we find that progressive democrats utilized democracy to mask setting up a socialist regime in Afghanistan. It is my belief that progressives wanted to have that stronghold to have strategic advantage in the Middle East to mobilize whatever they may need at the time. I do not believe at any time the progressives ever wanted to leave Afghanistan, which I believe President Trump had that deal set into place as a failsafe. Trump knew there was a chance he would lose the 2020 election, so he utilized his "American First" policy to justify pulling troops out of Afghanistan. Ghani was hand-picked by progressives, due to his matching ideology, in order to have an ally they could easily control when the progressive movement came to show their face. The problem with this grand scheme? Who are progressives? They are generally academics that lack the spine to do their dirty work, so they utilize strong, conservative military personnel that succeed at a high level under duress to achieve their goals. In current society, progressives overstocked their faith in progressive leadership and should have allowed room for more moderate democrats to be closer to the front lines. Hence the failure of Ghani. The moral of this story: when there is imminent adversity, a progressive will fall fast and seek hiding, such as the liberal morons on the West Coast hiding behind masks in order to prey on those weaker than them. It is amazing; however, when the real patriots show up to the battlefield, how quick these cowardly college academics find places to hide.

Other interests in Afghanistan revolve around illegal operations that directly affect our great nation. The number-one source of income for the Afghans is donations by other nations and private donors. You may ask why so many people have an interest in a mountainous desert? The second largest source of income, according to the BBC, is the drug trade. Opium is produced all over Afghanistan, and this plant is used to make heroin. So, it is very interesting that whenever the US is in a conflict in Southeast Asia, the heroin imports increase. It is easier to control the influx of drug trafficking when we are on the ground monitoring its production. Want to stop the heroin epidemic? Burn Afghanistan! In fact, we cannot, due to the US being the biggest drug dealers in the world. We can find Osama Bin Laden and Saddam Hussein, but we can't find large illegal drug manufacturers with the world's greatest intelligence community? Come on, we are not ignorant.

Another factor to consider as to the socialist agenda is Afghanistan's vast amount of mineral mining. According to the United States Geological Survey, Afghanistan has an estimated one trillion dollars' worth of unmined minerals. Ironically, in 2012, the Afghans began drilling for oil and natural gas, coming from oil industry tycoon George HW Bush, doesn't seem much of a coincidence. When you look at Afghanistan, it does now clearly set the stage for the vast wealth many countries will vie for now that the US is no longer available to control the region. I look for Russia, Iran, and China to lobby for their stake in the country's opium, oil, and gemstone industries. With the unstable government and lack of American commitment to back this nation going forward, a strong superpower country can easily come in and take their claim.

Concluding the Afghanistan conflict is not going to be easy for those committed American Patriots such as Ted Cruz and Jim Jordan. Currently, House Speaker Nancy Pelosi refuses to hear any motion brought before the House of Representatives regarding Afghanistan. President Joe Biden is guilty of gross neglect of United States citizens left behind and those soldiers killed. It is borderline, but I also believe his lack of leadership is going to be responsible for mass genocide of many Afghanistan's people that seek the American dream of democracy that they were promised. This is what happens when we have allowed a socialist regime to penetrate the heart of democracy. Our people need to wake up from being woke and see the mass oppression that is on the horizon. Do your own research and see the pattern from the Marxist playbook. The progressives are executing it masterfully without much resistance. This is our moment to push back and put a big dent in their plan. Our people left behind need avenged, and that is done with the impeachment of our weak president.

The aftermath of the debacle in Afghanistan is just as disturbing as the thoughtless event itself. It just seems there are not rights that happened at all and the whole withdrawal was a spontaneous, spur-of-the-moment decision by a leader or set of leaders that had no business making such a grand decision that would affect so many nations. If we match up the events of Afghanistan with the opinion polls that are constantly being collected, we can see that after the public deemed the pull-out a disaster, Biden and his Cabinet rooted around to find an answer the American public would positively respond to in the polls. It was adamantly apparent that what the American public wanted was for terrorists to die and the rest of our citizens to be brought home. On September 17th, the White House released the results from their drone strike that was purportedly targeted towards an alleged Isis-K operative but instead ended up being a family in a car. Those innocent people were murdered by a president that has no regard for human life of any kind. I am happy, however, that we are out of the country for the most part, so President Biden will not accidently drone strike more innocent Afghan citizens

Had this happened under President Trump, there would have been an immediate impeachment inquiry that would lead to a house vote, which in turn would likely lead to a Senate impeachment. No one on either side of the isle will allow for mass murder by generals that obviously either did not require ground intelligence or didn't care who perished in the drone strike. After all, it was only a publicity stunt to raise his approval rating, but Biden just can't seem to get it right. But what do we expect from a society that is in constant contradiction as to where our moral compass is pointing?

When you think the controversy is over and we can re-hash a plan to heal as a nation, Bob Woodward releases a book just in time to create issues over his commitment to the American Armed Services. Woodward is claiming that General Mark Milley made several phone calls to Chinese military commanders while he worked in the Trump Administration. President Trump has already made a statement that he was unaware of General Milley's involvement with any such conversations with China. If Bob Woodward's "anonymous" sources are accurate, this poses several imminent dangers to the ranks of our military. According to Woodward, General Milley made a phone call to Chinese General Li Zuocheng in order to warn him that President Trump may strike China, however, reassured the Chinese general that he would not allow anyone under his command fulfill any such orders by the Commander-in-Chief, President Trump.

The United States Constitution clearly states that someone charged with treason against the United States of America, "shall consist only in levying war against them, or in adhering to their enemies, giving them aid and comfort." If evidence is found against General Milley, he in fact should be charged with treason and face the potential penalties that a conviction would warrant. What he is accused of is giving comfort to our enemies behind the president's back. In the law of our great nation, only the president can give the order for military action. If true, General Milley indeed conducted in treasonous behavior and should no longer be trusted to lead our great military.

Also stated in our Constitution that may be an issue of receiving the proper conviction of General Milley is the continued Article III, section 3, clause 1, definition. It states that "No person shall be convicted of treason unless on the testimony of two witnesses to the same overt acts, or on confession in open court." Knowing how Bob Woodward never reveals his sources, it is likely not possible to bring those sources to light and to have others in our military, along with Biden's Administration, testify against General Milley, while implicating themselves. There is an alternate solution that we allow the military to court martial him, which upon conviction would likely end his career. In my opinion, when you add up all the atrocities of the Afghanistan debacle, with the allegations of treason, General Milley should be held responsible. We have more than enough dead soldiers and civilians to have him removed from command. If we leave judgement up to the White House, it is unlikely General Milley will face any reprimand.

The justice system needs to take any book written by Bob Woodward with a fine-tooth comb. He's an avid Trump basher, but plans the release of his book at a time when it enhances the damage to an already masterful disaster. I see two different motives for the release of this book. As Mark Levin stated on *Hannity*, 9-17-21, it takes a book several months for it to be ready to publish. What this is saying is, Bob Woodward held onto this information for at least two to three months. Most likely he has known about it for quite longer. In the coming months, I do hope we find out how long this highly sensitive information has been hidden from the public eye. Woodward did one of two things: He waited to release his book until the exact right time in order to hurt the Biden Administration at a time when they are already losing the trust of the American people. He also could have tried miserably to paint Milley as an American hero by standing up to President Trump and "preventing a large-scale war."

No one is perfect, as is there such thing as a perfect lie. If you sift back far enough, holes emerge. The problem with painting Milley as a hero is, either way you look at it, he failed protocol. We have in this country and Congress that deals with the power of the president, such as the Twenty-fifth Amendment. There were and still are enough tyrants in our Congress to where an immediate inquiry would have been started to limit Trumps war powers. As far as we know, no such inquiry was ever made. Milley did consult with House Speaker Nancy Pelosi. It is unclear as to what her recommendation was to General Milley, but Milley did speak to China is a way that the president was left in the dark, which would have dire circumstances for our troops had Trump took a military approach to China. What would have happened is our troops would have been slaughtered by China, as Milley gave them the strategic advantage of our attack. This is unacceptable in any court of law in our country. This is a huge problem that every American should be concerned about. Worst-case scenario, China is easily able to invade our country and stop at our doorstep. It is imperative we do not disclose our military strategy to anyone, let alone our enemies.

If the information in Woodward's book is less than accurate, he needs to be penalized and charged. In the sensitive nature of our country, the last thing we need is a rogue author issuing a *New York Times* bestseller about our military leaders falsely committing treason. The untruthful publication is more mammoth than what Bob Woodward realizes. Our enemies can read too. They will see more discord and separation than what we already emit to the world, which will eventually allow one of our enemies to eventually try our bravery and valor. And as of right now, I'm not sure our leadership can handle such conflict with a superpower after giving in to a much weaker Taliban.

September 28th became a sensitive day in Washington as General Milley, General McKenzie, and Secretary Austin testified before Congress over the rapid departure from Afghanistan. Most of the questioning from GOP members revolved around who is responsible for leaving Americans behind. General Milley took several questions about his interactions with a Chinese Military leader. House members were very forward and made it very clear that someone had to be held accountable, which Secretary Austin reassured the committee that the investigation is ongoing, and they hope to figure out who is going to be accountable, which, sarcastically, lets me sleep at night.

I spent a lot of time watching their testimonies and found a few things of note. Although General Milley, heading into the testimony, was the target of most of the verbal barrage GOP House members threw at the gentlemen being questioned due to his potential treasonous phone calls with Chinese officials, I felt Milley handled questioning very straightforward. Generally, people who lie have several tells that are usually easily seen by even the most amateur viewer. Milley appeared to be in control and direct, with very little stuttering or fidgeting. Without going over his testimony with a bunch of technological forensics equipment, he appeared to be genuine and honest. When asked about his suggestions to the president in reference to the Afghanistan departure, he did dodge a direct answer, while indirectly insinuating that President Biden did not heed his professional suggestions as to handle the situation.

General McKenzie, too, appeared to be honest and direct. Either these two generals are so good at lying in the exact same professional manner, or they are both being honest. There was no hesitation in their responses, and they seemed to have taken advantage of pointing the finger at the president. Defense Secretary Austin, however, struggled with several answers. He even, at times, justified not giving the Americans that were trapped there the priority they should have been given.

No matter what way we look at the Afghanistan withdrawal, thirteen American soldiers died in vain. I do not see how history will paint Biden for anything other than an incompetent quasi-leader for his lack of preparation in extracting all the correct personnel without a shot being fired. That is how it should have happened. This is what we get as Americans when we bring socialists into power, collateral damage in their eyes. We will not forget what you did, Mr. President.

CHAPTER 4

CHINA AND RUSSIA

There is a major rapid development going on in the world, and I believe it is aimed at the demise of the American Ideology. As President Biden emits a very weak leadership role among the world powers, look for other nations to take full advantage of the situation. It is very clear after the masterful failure of the retreat from Afghanistan and ignoring the kidnapped US aid workers in Haiti that President Biden is incapable and lacks the fortitude to protect the great people of our nation.

The people of the US need to understand a very key component of what's going on in the world that the media is missing, showing us the warning signs. Russia has been the boogeyman of Americans for many decades, and that world depiction has not let up much since then. Under President Vladimir Putin, Russia is a very dangerous country to be in a potential conflict. On 4-13-17, President Trump, in his quest to eliminate ISIS, dropped a devastating MOAB (mother of all bombs) strike on ISIS terrorists in Afghanistan. This bomb was the first time the US had dropped an explosive of that magnitude since the nuclear retaliation from Japan's attack on Pearl Harbor. In response to the US MOAB launch, 9-12-17 Russia dropped their FOAB (father of all bombs) on Syrian ISIS terrorist. In point, Russia is not afraid to get into a who's bigger competition with American.

Current relations have not improved over the years, even through the Trump Presidency. The left utilized false information from the Steele Dossier to attempt to tie Trump to Russia, which was found as a tactic to create lack of trust and discredit Trump in his first year in the White House. Blaming Russia for every mishap in our nation is a grave mistake. I commend President Trump for his attempts to create peace and generate international relations with Russia, which is rich in several natural resources that the US could benefit from. Instead, both the left and right utilize Nazi-style media propaganda to push a Russia is the ultimate bad-guy scenario but ignore more nations that pose just as much or more of a threat to our national security.

We have been seeing an ongoing act and react game out of the US and Russia that has now filtered to several European countries. Russia will send fighter jets or bombers close to Alaskan borders, and US fighter jets will chase them off. On the reverse side, US and English warships will come a little too close to Russian waters, and their navy and air force will chase them away. There is a definitive reason for all the nitpicking on these borders. As the US publicly avoids fault with anything that has anything to do with Russia, it is evident that intelligence will continue to monitor their movements, and rightly so.

American forces have not been involved in any known gunfight with Russia or aggressive military maneuvers, but I feel that is coming to a head very soon. Before the invasion of the Ukraine, while in a standoff with the Russians on the Russia/Ukraine border over terri-tory boundaries, so we initially believed, Russia began putting their pieces in play. On 11-3-21, the *Associated Press* reported that Russia has around ninety thousand troops on the border ready to invade the Ukraine. Several days later, Secretary Blinkin released a statement in-directly threatening Russia against a Russian invasion of Ukraine. It is my opinion, based on actions of the Biden Administration, that Rus-sia was calling America's bluff at the time, which proved to be true. If US forces assist the Ukraine, it would create a huge issue of priority for Biden as he abandons trapped Americans all over the world just to pick up and help a nation that is rich in corruption and ties to, wait, Hunter Biden!

Continuing, in early December Russia administered more aggressive behavior with the Ukraine, citing the UN to release a series of threats of sanctions. In the US, while wokeism raged across our nation, Press Secretary Psaki found time to administer empty sanction threats towards Putin if he makes a move against Ukrainian troops on their border. The standoff proves that all it will take to have a chaotic series of events that will likely cause the largest multinational war our planet has ever seen would be one bad decision by an incompetent leader.

My belief previously was that when Russia and the Ukraine started their conflict, it would have started the invasion of Taiwan by China. Biden would have had to make a decision to either engage China or Russia or both. Either way, this is going to be a major disaster that will have catastrophic results not only for the world but the US. These conflicts are all distractions that have been carefully plotted for years by Vladimir Putin and Xi Jing Ping. We need to never underestimate these two leaders. They have total control of their situations and are strategically light years ahead of our distracted administration. When you want to be king of the world and have the opportunity to overthrow an empire while its weak, you seize the opportunity. That is the situation that we are in right now.

When we observe on the outside what is taking place in the world, it is easy to see the conflicts brewing. It is my opinion that there is an even larger picture. What I hope our military leaders are seeing is the placement of the Chinese and Russian military. It is very clear to me that Putin and Xi have a very close alliance and are ready to exploit our strategic weakness. According to a freedom of information request by Ezra Levant, a Canadian Journalist, Canada had allowed China to come to their country to see how they train for winter warfare. This is not just a simple cross-training of friendly countries as the US would do with England. What occurred, along with other underlying scenarios, is a show of loyalty by the Canadians with our foe, China.

Canada is not the only country that China has their hands buried deep into. Mexico and China have many non-red-flag bearing relationships; however, with the large and very open US-Mexican border, it appears China has a very resourceful ally that can give them a very strong military advantage. This happened due to China's economic stronghold on the world. China shows up at everyone's doorstep with a deal that no one can pass up in the international commerce world. Struggling countries such as Mexico and anything else south of our neighbor will take this deal, as opposed to doing business with the US due to China's reluctance to "play by the rules" as the rest of the common players of the world do. China basically undercuts every world competitor with just slightly less quality. Their financial influence is buried deep into Mexico and Central America.

Cuba is an interesting and longtime ally of China as Fidel Castro built his regime based off the Chinese Communist playbook. As I'm seeing this all unfold, it appears that Cuba has been a strategic puppet for decades in wait for the perfect opportunity for China to call their debt. I believe that time is among us in present day. In July of 2020, Cuban commoners took to the streets to protest their government's handling of the COVID pandemic. The people were left to starve and left without necessities. It made me wonder, as the refugees tried to flee, why Biden did not open the border to rescue these severely oppressed peoples. Instead, he offered them the Internet. That is a huge joke. These people need refuge, not Wi-Fi. Then just as fast as the uprising happened, it disappeared from the American Media. What occurred is that China cut all access to the outside world from the Cuban people. Without a tech voice for the Cuban people, they would just fade away into the silence of their government. It is likely that the Chinese helped the Cuban Government hunt down the insurrectionists and had them jailed or worse.

Take a simple look at what is taking place; Russia and China are both taking strategic stances against two countries they can conquer in ten minutes, prompting the rest of the world to pay attention to those specific areas. This is simply a divide-and-conquer method that world leaders have been falling for for centuries, and the US will likely follow suit. Russia and China have been participating in war game preparation close to the Alaskan border off and on for years. China has a distinct strategic alliance placement with nearly every country surrounding the US. My theory is, war breaks out in the Ukraine, NATO, along with the US, eventually jumps in to help, then China invades Taiwan with a smaller force that is expendable. When half the forces shift their focus to Taiwan, China and Russia invade the US on four fronts. They come in the West Coast, Canada, Mexico, and the Caribbean via Cuban military.

I like to look at the numbers game, and when you see who's in conflict with who and who has the upper hand, the New Axis Powers have the upper hand in numbers. China, Russia, Cuba, and new Axis power India have a combined total of 4,704,178 active-duty military personnel, with an additional 5,125,000 in reserve for a total of 9,829,178 total troops at their expense. The Ally side of things with the US, Ukraine, NATO, Taiwan, and Australia have 5,289,060 active-duty military personnel, while having 1,959,500 in reserve for a total of 7,248,560 to utilize. It is easy to see how this will turn out if conflict ends up in a ground-and-pound conflict.

When you look at breaking up the forces based on interest in specific conflicts, the New Allies on the Ukrainian front, which consist of the US, NATO, and the Ukraine, can amass 3,977,950 against a Russian force that can round up 3,013,628 ground troops. Man versus man, this should be a victory for the Ally forces.

Meanwhile, in Taiwan, the numbers game appears close to this; the Allied countries of the US, NATO, Taiwan, and Australia can provide 3,358,583 troops on the ground, while Axis countries of China can amass 4,115,000. This man-versus-man scenario would appear to be a catastrophic loss for the Allied countries.

There are several other factors to consider when these series of events take place, with the biggest being will Ally forces deploy all troops at 100 percent? The answer is no, they won't. NATO has troops stationed all over the world, while redeploying these troops to Taiwan or the Ukraine would surely open conflict in the areas abandoned. To say the Allied forces will provide all the military personnel in the above data is highly unlikely. What we have learned about Russia, especially from their behavior in WWII, their people will come together to fight in unity against any enemy as they did in Germany. I would expect Russian military numbers to be much greater than what is reported in a time of great conflict. The US is also in a situation where if they abandon all their bases abroad, large conflicts will emerge from where they left, so the likelihood of the US numbers being at full strength are a stretch as well.

Much will be the same in China, when looking at the imminent invasion of Taiwan. China will send everything they have and likely defeat whomever stands in their way, due to an overpowering of forces and assets in proximity of the small island of Taiwan. It is a high probability that this war will be fought over open water in between China and Taiwan, which China has the upper hand due to their naval and air force access.

Other factors to consider in this clear disaster for the US is the role India will play in conflict in both Taiwan and Ukraine. In December of 2021, President Putin met with Indian President Ram Nath Kovind regarding having co-op military drills for what reason? India, for many years, has had an up-and-down relationship with US leaders, which has caused dissent amongst the two powerful nations. I see India seizing their opportunity to do their part to end the US control of the world. The next factor to pay close attention to is what will Iran and North Korea do while NATO and the US are distracted by several wars going on? I predict many nations will take advantage of a weakened US military to attain their own agenda.

World leaders should be concerned for several reasons; however, what should be noted the most is what we don't see on the surface in surefire naval battles among both conflicts. Submarine battles are going to matter exponentially, and Ally nations are at a huge disadvantage. The US have reported sixty-eight subs, while China has seventy-nine, Russia has sixty-four, North Korea has thirty-six, Iran has twenty-nine, and India has seventeen. I'm no math wizard but all the wrong countries have a devastating number of submarines compared to Axis countries. This is going to prove to be a huge problem.

In mid-2021, Russia and China both revealed their hypersonic missiles that can carry nuclear warheads. US military leaders claimed they had no idea that either country could manufacture that kind of technology. Well, surprise, it's here, and no other country has anything that can shoot those missiles down before entire cities are destroyed. No missile defense system known to the public has the capabilities to protect their land anymore. If either Russia or China deploy hypersonic missiles, it will be checkmate and we need to get out our Rosetta Stone software because we will all be speaking Russian and Mandarin.

Wokeism is the last factor to consider. Our military is not mentally prepared to handle several significant conflicts abroad. Our soldiers are too worried about not offending each other to realize race and sexual orientation are not the real problems. China and Russia are. In warfare, America as adopted an avoid inhumanity policy while the cameras are rolling during war issues. Russia and China will not fight according to the rules of engagement. They will carpet bomb and napalm anything they want to, and there is no amount of sanctioning that will change that, because, in the end, once they defeat the Allied forces, there will be no larger body of international government that can enforce anything on them.

As tensions continue to burn like a well-lit campfire, Russia appears likely they are going to invade the Ukraine by the end of January. With the amount of military equipment the US and European countries have provided the Ukraine, they appear to be better equipped and properly trained to hold their front against a much more advanced Russian force. When Russia recovered the Crimean Peninsula from the Ukraine, Ukrainian forces did not seem to put up much of a fight. It does seem to appear that this conflict is not going to be a walk in the park for Russia.

President Biden, for some reason, keeps placing himself and the US in the middle of the conflict, which I feel is not our war. I believe this move by the Biden Administration is clearly a political maneuver to help a family acquaintance. The biggest issue that Biden's involvement is causing is, Putin does not take him seriously, and neither does any country on the planet right now. President Biden, outside of British Prime Minister Boris Johnson, is the laughingstock of the world. There is a reason we are not hearing admitted public support for the president or his administration. Jen Psaki has become the democrats voice of nothing. At the end of the day, everyone jumps off the sinking ship, and with Biden's continual tanking poll numbers, which he claims are fake, the Democrat Party is headed for a lot more disappointment.

With Biden's credibility and attempt at stern threats in question, I do not think Putin will stop his agenda to invade the Ukraine. 2022 started out as a relatively quiet year for the China/Taiwan conflict. I feel this is due to the Russia/Ukraine conflict. The whole world was distracted by what Putin was doing on the Ukrainian border while China is in wait like a snake in the grass. When Putin invaded, China should have started their hostile takeover of Taiwan. It is a perfect military strategy. Let your flunky do the work you don't want to do while you do the easier route. Taiwan will fall quickly with not much international help as the Russia/Ukraine conflict will prove to be long and bloody. Strategically, it is a perfect storm that emulates the chaos theory a bit. When we take a step back and really diagnose international conflicts during the Biden Administration, it is evident that Xi Jinping has out maneuvered the world's greatest leaders.

In mid-January 2022, as tensions between the Ukraine and Russia grew to a boiling point as to where an invasion is more and more likely, China sent thirty-nine war planes into Taiwanese airspace. This was either a real time drill to prepare or a strong act of aggression. It appears the timing of this maneuver was very strategic, as China was using the distraction of the Russia/Ukraine conflict to their advantage. It is very absurd that when I watch social media or mainstream news, no one is talking about what is occurring between the two conflicts. Russia/Ukraine is not the biggest problem we are about to face, China is. It is terrifying because Americans doesn't see what's happening, and I don't believe President Biden is in reality enough to make a solid decision as to how to come out on top in the power-changing event that I believe will eventually happen.

February of 2022 brought forth a lot of confusion in the Balkan region, as Russia and Belarus claimed to be merely exercising war games together and not an invasion on the Ukraine. As NATO and Washington still insist that Russia was going to invade at any day, nothing had happened that suggested an invasion was on the brink. I believe that Putin was playing games and is intellectually leagues ahead of all world leaders on the planet. I believe this is a huge diversion for something much bigger than a war over the Ukraine.

Justification is a big deal in international policy, almost as much as honoring a treaty. In 1991, the Washington Treaty among NATO nations produced an agreement that says, "NATO would not expand into territory east of Germany." Clearly, looking at a map, we can see that that region is what we know as the Balkans, which includes the Ukraine. For NATO to assemble even one soldier past the German border would be a violation of the Washington Treaty, NATO's founding document. What this does is creates justification for an invasion caused by the belief of a broken treaty. NATO is not as popular in Europe as we would like to think they are as Americans whose government dumps excessive money into without return. Agreements are agreements, and the one large issue that is at stake is that NATO is going to cause Germany to lose their Nordstream 2 pipeline deal that is in place with Russia. This is significant as Europe struggles and depends on several Asian countries to provide natural resources to heat their homes and fuel their cars. As of the last week of February 2022, Germany has not answered NATO's call for troops, as they understand that fighting a country that is crucial to their survival is not wise.

On February 24th, 2022, Russia did in fact invade the Ukraine. Putin sent forces from Russia and Belarus from the north, east, and south from Crimea. On paper it appeared that Putin would quickly conquer the Ukraine; however, the Ukrainian people have come together and have created some momentum by having some small wins against a trained killing machine. As over three million Ukrainians have fled west to Poland, many nationalists have stayed to fight as President Volodymyr Zelenskyy passed a decree where males between the ages of eighteen to sixty are required to stay in the country and bear arms against the Russian invaders.

While the invasion is important, I have a hard time getting past the lack of preventative measures that could have deterred this growing bloodbath of innocent Ukrainians. President Putin has been very transparent as to what he was planning as far as intentions in the Ukraine. President Biden in turn utilized a reactive stance, which is a huge mistake. After NATO nations and the US issued a long list of sanctions against Russia, it changed nothing as it comes to stopping the invasion. Instead, we have observed a huge gas hike at the pumps, energy rates jump along with natural gas. Since Biden took away our own ability to produce our own energy in mass, Putin took control of the world energy markets. Yes, Putin has been planning to take back the Ukraine for a very long time; however, it was going to take the right US president to achieve this task. America lacks toughness and heart among our leadership, which is prime for a major world bully like Putin to come in and attempt to achieve one phase of his legacy.

Have you ever talked to that guy after witnessing a fight between two other people, he always says, "I would have kicked his ass," but he never gets involved or has anything to say to either culprit's face? That is NATO and the US in this situation. If you're not going to step in and fight, then get the hell out of here. The sanctions are not saving Ukrainian children, which should be looked at as a crime against humanity. The fact is, NATO is afraid of Russia. The US is afraid of Russia. It is very disturbing how, a few years ago, every nation considered Ukraine as too corrupt to admit into NATO. But today we glorify the very corrupt tyrant that we previously criticized. From my bird nest, this war is no one's business except Russia and Ukraine, as both countries are led by devious leaders. After all, we didn't seem to care when China murdered many Uyghurs.

By the third day of battle and the closing in on Kiev, several parliament members propagated to American media news outlets for the US to stop sanctions and instead patrol the airspace over the Ukraine. What this does is places the US namely into a conflict with Russia, which I'm not sold that we can really win. Instead, we have world leaders on TV every night talking about the fight but doing nothing about it. Let the two brothers fight it out. President Biden is clearly doing what he has proven himself to be an expert in, failure.

In the meantime, China invaded Taiwanese airspace for the first time in decades and will be conducting war games off the coast of Taiwan. I'm hopeful the White House is not going to be as passive on developments between China and Taiwan. Russia is a distraction and strategic observing by China. Russia needs to keep the Ukrainian conflict moving slowly and tirelessly until China goes into Taiwan. China clearly will have the upper hand, as they have seen the US and Europe stand on the sidelines as cheerleaders for a football game. Putin doesn't care about sanctions because China is financing Russia, while India refuses to accept the American dollar in support of Russia. My question next is, how is Biden going to back out of a conflict with China? This is becoming his modus operendi.

It is amazing as to how American media was so distracted by the Ukraine-Russia war that they have not mentioned the Chinese Air Force entering Taiwanese air space for the first time in decades. The act was a very aggressive show of force which should have been noted among international powers. The media's lack of dereliction for the Chinese military movements is a travesty. We have been duped and misdirected.

Just like the Ukraine, Taiwan has no real international memberships that obligates nations to assist them against China. What the Ukraine-Russian war told China is that when a big dog shows up, no one is going to help the little country. This poses a huge international problem across the board. The evils of the world now have a cheat code that allows them to maneuver strategically without much resistance from outside forces.

One aspect to consider when it comes to picking and choosing which opponent to take seriously, Russia, in proximity to all of Europe, is an immediate threat not only in comparison to ground force accessibility but also in the nuclear race. According to Businessinsider.com, Russia has around 6,255 warheads, which is more that China and the US put together. It is estimated that China has between 200–350 warheads. It would be a good assessment that Taiwan is not going to be a big enough fish to nuke, as China would merely need to only put a small portion of their military on the ground to take the island, where the Ukraine is a little more complicated and political, which make the world place more emphasis on the conflict in the Ukraine.

As the Russia strategically maneuvers around Ukrainian cities at the beginning of March 2022, mainstream media has temporarily abandoned the theory that President Putin has gone mad. Instead, they are seeing his strategy play out to make a lot of sense. I believe Putin knew that the Ukrainians would put up a valiant fight against any Russian aggression. Putin also knew that Russia is the nuclear king of the world, and therefore, he has the upper hand in negotiations, while keeping Ukrainian sympathizers at bay due to the fear of being nuked.

Putin also has the angle of time. The longer this conflict goes on with sanctions, the weaker the US economy gets, inflation goes up, gas goes up, and all utilities will become more expensive. While the West and Europe believe their governmental bodies are punishing Putin, in fact they are punishing themselves. What does not add up to me is how is Russia supposed to become broke and unable to continue financing war when Biden and Europe are still buying Russian oil? In the global market, when you buy something, you are obligated to pay for it, so it appears that Putin is not really going broke; in fact, it seems that he is continuing the economic pace that initially allowed him to fund the war in the first place. I am led to believe that the US-NATO cheerleading team is rooting for small potatoes, when the much larger sanctions would be to boycott Russian oil and produce our own for ourselves and global customers. This would destroy Russia's ability to make a penny. Instead, the sanctions in place are largely only robbing the Russian wealth of their assets while they are overseas. To me, that is not accomplishing much.

I still go back to Putin's initial explanation as to why he first went into the Donetsk and Luhansk regions of the Ukraine. According to Putin, Ukrainian military had been attacking Ukrainian and Russian citizens and separatists in their respective regions. As the death toll began to rise, Putin decided that since President Zelenskyy refused to stop the attacks, he would be forced to intervene and officially declare Donetsk and Luhansk their own sovereign states. The more and more I investigate this claim, the more it makes sense, as both of the regions border Russia, and, geographically, I would give a solid assumption that there are many families that are divided into both Russian and Ukrainian citizenship. Some of those families are going to support the Russian way of life, while some are going to side more with the Ukrainian government.

Mainstream European and Western US media refuse to acknowledge the Ukrainian military killing separatist and civilians. On March 5th, 2022, *Russia Today* reported a story involving a Russian Olympic synchronized swimmer named Marina Goliadkina. Goliadkina was in fact born and raised in the Donetsk region and claims that "Russians stepped in to stand up for" the region. Goliadkina goes on to say, "I was there under shelling in 2014. I saw how people killed their own. Everyone knew how citizens in Donbass were bombed, literally exterminating people." It is apparent that there is a very interesting side of Ukraine that, for political purposes, is not being told. The five-time world champion finished by stating, "I felt this war. And today I clearly understand who takes part in it. It is a pity that the world community did not raise so much noise for the citizens of Donetsk and Lugansk all these years, for whom Russia had the courage to stand up. It is as if the people who used to live in Donbass have forgotten what happened there, and as if this war did not hurt anyone."

These statements come from a Ukrainian woman that fled a war-torn area that the world courts do not want to acknowledge. To paint Russia as the bad guy fits the West political agenda more that avenging an Eastern Ukrainian slaughter of average citizens. I have also noticed that even Fox News will not interview anyone in the Eastern Ukraine. Media coverage pretty much goes from Kiev and on to the west, as if the Eastern Ukrainians are not there to be heard.

If we do not pay close attention to the agenda of China, while Putin keeps our coffers distracted with the oil industry and free handouts of large sums of cash to the Ukraine, we are going to be in big trouble. I surely hope someone in that White House has a plan that will work.

CHAPTER 5

SOCIALISM

For decades, our country has been infiltrated by Marxists, socialists, and Communists. We have been fighting them off, and they keep coming back. We look at what is currently happening in the democratic party. When you hear the word progressive democrat, that is just a politically correct way to say socialist. I remember the first time I heard the term progressive, when Hillary Clinton was running for the presidential nomination against Barak Obama. At the time I had no idea what that meant, nor did I realize the power of that single word in our government, so I discarded the constant reference Clinton made to herself. The progressives in our country have been trying and failing to subdue our will to this agenda, but the words communism and socialism just doesn't sit well with the American people on either side of the isle.

Since the early '90s, the socialists have been slowly acquiring power bit by bit, and it wasn't until Bernie Sanders' failed bid to become president that they realized they may have their best shot to fully overturn our capitalist democracy, which they are anti. Sanders' popularity among the college-age Americans gave the democrats hope for the future; however, his sudden and unexpected surge in popularity likely cost Hillary Clinton the presidency in 2016. We all know a divided party is a failed party.

One fact that Americans do not know is that former president Barak Obama was an active associate of the American Communist Party at the University of Chicago. This affiliation and his dedication to its methodology allowed him to stand out and become a powerful figure in the Chicago area. Obama, in fact, was an excellent public figure and speaker. His message was believable, and he appeared to bring people together, including the urban African American communities. In his message, he pressed change, which I think every American can agree we needed drastically at that time as career normal politicians were just not getting it done anymore.

The problem Obama faced was simple. He never followed through in helping minority groups achieve the success he promised. Change never happened, instead the opposite, Americans experienced the worst depression since the Great Depression. This is what happens when you raise corporate taxes, jobs move out of the country, and unemployment goes up. Capitalism is a very easy concept when you look at the basis of what it is: have a competitive corporate tax rate and jobs will stay and arrive in hoards, have the import and export capabilities and allow for tax breaks. Without corporate tax breaks, jobs will move overseas in order to save millions of dollars. This occurs because if Walmart is more expensive than Publix, you're going to stop shopping at Walmart. Americans are dollar stretchers; we want more bang for our buck. This is no different in corporate America. For example, President Trump's corporate tax rate was set at a flat 21 percent. Joe Biden wants to raise it to 28 percent. This is a 7 percent increase that costs corporations millions, if not billions of dollars a year in lost revenue. I cannot speak for every corporation, but the company I work for trickled that money down to the floor workers. We saw our most generous raises under Trump's tax plan.

You may ask, why still leave America? According to Tax Foundation, the average corporate tax rate of the twenty-seven European Union countries is 21.47 percent. This is an area that is fantastic for import and export. President Trump had Americans right at that rate, which is competitive. At 28 percent, America will move closer to the bottom rankings of the world tax rates. Central America is even lower than what Biden wants to set us at. If I own a corporation, I for sure will shop my rates, just like insurance, and see who has the best tax rate for my company, which will generate more money for me and my workers.

Second question is, why do the democrats not get it? This is because of the socialist movement. Socialism defined by Oxford means, "a political and economic theory of social organization which advocates that the means of production, distribution, and exchange should be owned or regulated by the community as a whole." In layman's terms, work a job with skill or one with none and you will be given rations by your community (government) at intervals directed by the community. Nothing more, nothing less. So, your PhD isn't worth the paper it's written on. For all of you blind liberals not reading between the lines, you're going to be oppressed like other socialist countries such as Cuba, current Afghanistan, North Korea, Venezuela, etc. It is astounding at how many videos are on YouTube about protests that are pro-socialism. Makes me sick. I didn't work this hard to have my hard work taken away from me by a government machine that sees me as an ant in an ant farm.

Socialism is happening everyday right in front of our faces. We are just half immune to it because the progressives are not specifically calling it socialism. This does not change what the agenda is. Leftist agendas are clearly derived from a socialist playbook that is headed by an unknown assailant that is out of the public eye somewhat. I feel that there are political faces of the agenda such as Chuck Schumer, Nancy Pelosi, Jen Psaki, Alexandria Ocasio-Cortez, and Bernie Sanders. Hillary Clinton is also a key figure in the cog that has been created by what I believe is one culprit. I can only be theoretical as to whom that benefactor is, but I have my suspicion.

George Soros seems to be the Oz behind the curtain to many institutions and people that can instill his ideology that he is the king of the world. Soros, however, is an aging ninety-one-year-old Hungarian that I feel is spending whatever it takes to have one last shot to own the United States. When you read about George Soros on Wikipedia, they clearly state that Republicans paint the billionaire as a "puppet master" of many global situations. Obviously, the liberal-leaning Wikipedia has a clear bias as you can follow Soros's money around and find that he is in fact buying people and institutions to complete his narrative.

One of the prime sources of spreading money all over the world by Soros is his Open Society Foundation, formerly headquartered out of Budapest, Hungary, currently based in Berlin, Germany. The OSF is so controversial that in 2018, the Hungarian government passed legislation to launch a massive investigation into the OSF. OSF has several angles as part of what they distribute funds to. One very interesting fact is their belief that the US should have open borders. As Biden continues to ignore the gaping issue due to his open border policy. It does make a bit of sense as to why Biden refuses to address the growing disaster at our nations border.

DCleaks released a document obtained from OSF that states, "For a variety of reasons, we wanted to construct a diversified portfolio of grants dealing with Israel and Palestine, funding both Israeli Jewish and PCI (Palestinian Citizens of Israel) groups as well as building a portfolio of Palestinian grants and in all cases to maintain a low profile and relative distance-particularly on the advocacy front." When I diagnose this release, I see a foundation that is not advocating for peace but an organization that is funding the conflict to continue. Further review suggests that OSF is funding the opposition of Israeli prosperity even though Soros himself is of Jewish descent. OSF's agenda is also set on placing distance between the US and Israel, which, when we look at how our elected officials view and speak out against our oldest ally, Israel, it does not seem to make sense as to why Soros, as a Jew, would turn his back on his faith system. He does not consider himself a Zionist, but Jewish faith does seem to be a generations-long-running system in his family. What I feel has happened, Soros became powerful through the fortune he accumulated, and became bigger than the Jewish faith. The abundant evidence and how he portrays himself on the world stage, along with the tentacles he has in so many people of world power, indicate he firmly believes he is larger than life.

OSF doesn't appear to have a national ally but does seem to have plenty of enemies globally. Even Russia treads away from anything that has Soros's name attached to it. In 2015, Russian authorities found "the activity of the Open Society Foundations and the Open Society Institute Assistance Foundation represents a threat to the foundations of the constitutional system of the Russian Federation and the security of the state." Granted, Russia is very strategic and cautious as to what they allow to have happen in their country, which they have their own agenda politically, but it does confirm that the OSF is not a sweet and innocent organization that mainstream media wants you to think they are. Further, OSF and other acronym agencies with Soros's fingerprints on it are banned in several countries, such as in Russia, Romania, Hungary, Poland, Macedonia, Pakistan, and Turkey.

The claim that OSF is a philanthropy, scholarship, and grant organization is a complete half-farse. After searching the web to find information as to what neutral parties OSF has donated to, it comes back as a goose egg. Instead, I find oodles of information of propaganda made by left media about how much of a stand-up guy Soros is. It seems as you follow the monetary path of OSF and George Soros, you will find that he is sticking solely to a more sinister plot to complete his socialist agenda, which he is not keeping very well hidden in our society.

Daniel Bessner of the *Guardian* wrote a one-sided but very informative piece on how Soros is highly misunderstood and has been turned into the boogeyman by the right. This is what socialist countries have done to us, with the help of mass media Hitleresque propaganda method while anyone that digs too much and finds out what is happening as delusional fanatics. Bessner claims that republicans have "surprisingly little interest in what he actually thinks." I don't need to be manipulated by an obvious billionaire that puts human life behind his thirst to turn the world into a socialist empire of oppression with the delusion that we are going to live in utopia. Every socialist leader sells the same story: follow me to the great utopian hippie society but don't look at the part where I idolize the leaders and authors that support societies where the population is violently oppressed. Except for present China, this plan has never worked in history. Every communist or socialist nation falls miserably.

Further stated, Bessner asserts Soros is "a provocative and consistent thinker committed to pushing the world in a cosmopolitan direction in which racism, income inequality, American empire, and the alienations of contemporary capitalism would be things of the past. He is extremely perceptive about the limits of markets and US power in both domestic and international contexts. He is, in short, among the best meritocracy has produced." After all the fancy ass-kissing and positive word play that's throughout Bessner's article is the true agenda of Soros. To dissect what is a very good attempt to word play a dangerous man, there is more than what meets the eye. I don't think anyone is opposed to racial equality. Both sides of the aisle seem to be in agreeance as to racism. Regardless of what left-leaning media claims about the right, they are just as for racial equality as the left. It's a no-brainer. What sticks out to me is the above quote from Soros's semi-biography about income inequality. This is a vast trick that all dictators throw out to the masses to get the lower class on board. This also links with his thoughts on eliminating capitalism. There are two types of lower-class citizens: those that are trying and just stuck in a mudhole they can't get out of, and there are those that are okay living their life off the government. Those are the people that have nothing to lose, and allowing them to fight for their free government handouts becomes a very powerful tool. Eliminating the middle class, as to what Soros is trying to do, will cause the fall of the American Dream and the freedom to succeed. Without our drive to succeed, we lose our souls, which makes dictators obtain national power without opposition until an uprising occurs.

George Soros is an evil man that has the next generation of his family set up to finish his agenda. If he achieves this, the world will be a highly controlled video game to the controllers of the world. It will be a world where we cannot advance forward. Personally, I am too much of a free-spirited person that strives for individual success in order to improve the quality of my family status, so having the government restrict my success is not going to work for me. I'd like to believe that the majority of Americans will feel the same way.

As Americans, we are bound by the blood of our ancestors to protect individual rights outlined by the US Constitution. If we fall short of that, we are the great failures in the eyes of our Founding Fathers, while every sacrifice, every death of an American by the hand of our international enemies past and present will be in vain. I propose a strong backlash to all known socialists in our country, private citizens to government officials that have tainted our national existence. I do believe that, in the end, America will naturally purge itself from every traitor and tyrant within our borders.

Americans need to be aware of the signs that socialism is in fact infiltrating our political and economic systems. The basis of socialism is public ownership. According to a CBS poll, 41 percent of Americans have a positive view of socialism. This number is astounding and shows how good of a job radicals have done at glorifying the Democratic Party into believing socialism is a great system America should follow. The basis of socialism revolves around making everything public or "common ownership." When you read these words, it seems fishy, but not evil. This is a typical left-wing word play tactic that socialists are known for. What it is really being said is that the government will own your property, and nothing will belong to you.

Socialism is anti-capitalism, so expect your small business to be highly restricted by the government, and they can alter your business as they see fit. In most socialist nations, the business will profit share to the government and decide how much your ration will be. Their anti-capitalism approach is a trick that takes the American dream of being financially stable in life and giving their hard work to that government to utilize in the free market. The money made off your money will not be returned back to you but instead be placed in fund the government will utilize at their leisure. In summary, if you are a manufacturer of any goods that the government deems useful to society's needs, you will be taken over.

What happens is an equal dispersing of rations to everyone in the country, with the exception of those classified as too cool for school, like oligarchs. If America does fall into the radical socialism spectrum, as the left is trying to do, there will be several individuals that will be exempt from participating in the rations giving. Do you really see Jeff Bezos and Warren Buffet giving up their businesses to government control in exchange for minor rations? This will not happen, as they will create some sort of oligarch classification like what occurs in Russia.

Investopedia.com gives an interesting depiction defining ownership under socialism. "Socialists contend that shared ownership of resources and central planning provide a more equal distribution of goods and services and a more equitable society." The word equitable appears to be the socialist campaign word throughout this movement. It's used in such a negative light as to what Democrats are utilizing it that hearing it makes my blood boil. Equitable, in misdirected leftist wordplay, means everyone will be treated the same, which is okay in that sense. It further means even your money, housing, occupation, and retirement will be the same. The average American will forfeit their right to succeed at their pace and passion. One percent club Democrats love the idea as they will be the classified oligarchs, and rations will not apply to them, and they will be free to participate in capitalism.

Socialism prevents the 99 percent from achieving oligarch status and will forever be compared to the commoner of medieval England, while Nancy Pelosi and Chuck Schumer achieve noble status. Those of you 99 percent dreamer Americans need to really take a long look as to how socialism works in comparison to what the Democrats are tricking us to migrate into. It is an obvious power grab and recertification of what America will represent in the future. We need to wake our college kids up and educate them as to what socialism will do to their futures. We need to wake up our minority groups as to what socialism means to their fight for equality in a country that should be free. Make no mistake, Democrats are working very hard for the next big scheme to strip us of another right that we are born or naturalized with. Do you really think all 150 million Democrats are going to be included in the master plan? Who are the puppets that are going to be left behind?

There are several countries in Europe that have adopted socialist governments and have or currently succeeded. After reviewing where the money goes and how we grade these countries, it is very easy to see why these certain governments are achieving a level of success. According to insidermonkey.com, the top five socialist nations are

5. Iceland
4. Norway
3. Finland
2. Denmark
1. Sweden

There are some similarities among these countries when we take a deep look at their socialist structures. All five have a competitive world market, as they are within the top thirty nations in the world. All five have moderate populations. With much more populous nations, it would be much more difficult to evenly disperse the national wealth to the masses. In the Nordic countries they are competitive enough in the world market to cover all the costs of their people. All five nations also have a firm grip on their crime rate. These countries are ranked very high on the safest countries to live in on earth, with Iceland ranked number one.

With national tyrants like Elizabeth Warren, Bernie Sanders, and AOC leading the socialist way, they have overlooked several grave errors in their strategic plan that Nordic socialist nations built their successes on. US crime is out of control, while the top five socialist countries have a vast and present law enforcement presence, Democratic socialists want to dismiss the idea of law and order. Our national melting pot is much too vast to accommodate everyone's individuality, which in turn creates socioeconomic oppression. America would have to dramatically downsize their ethnic groups in order to isolate people of the same ideals, which would allow for keeping the national happiness rate high, which leads to less crime.

The next major factor the left is omitting are the means to fund the nation. As the leaders of the world economy, for now, we have a major influence on how and when the world economy shifts here and there. What every leftist leader the US has had since Bill Clinton, they have squabbled the US markets. Their methodology for generating national wealth in comparison to socialistic ques are more at par with Venezuela or Cuba, rather than the Nordic nations. For the US to achieve what the Nordic socialist countries are achieving, we would have to vastly oppress the high majority of this country, which will not go well with anyone. America sees the trick Socialist Democrats are trying to pull on the people. Anyone that is still serving the socialist agenda, needs to really step back and look at what will happen to this country if we were to head down that road. Bernie Sanders wants us to think we are heading towards a Nordic way of socialism; instead, we will end up more like Cuba.

My theory as to how socialist Democrats plan to fund their change in government is by printing more money. With so many left-wing political leaders being of wealth, it makes no sense to me as to how they can make more money out of nowhere in order to sustain society. It cannot happen this way, as we are seeing in real time. Joe Biden printed a trillion dollars to fund the infrastructure bill and, boom, inflation skyrockets. With inflation over 8 percent, the 3 percent annual average wage increase is not enough. To keep people afloat, companies need to increase their own wages across the board to stay competitive in the job market. However, if they don't increase wages, they will lower their standard for obtaining a skilled worker. When company A raises wages, they will take an unexpected loss in their profit margins, which will render a higher mark up for their products. Inflation could turn into a never-ending cycle of increases if the wrong leadership were in power, which, currently, is the case.

Another quick comparison between the Nordic socialist countries and what Sanders thinks America needs to be is the fact that even though socialists in our country believe capitalism is the enemy, our country will still be capitalist when it comes to international trade. Nordic nations understand this and have adjusted to being capitalists. We refer to Cuba again, and they're not well known in the international trade community, and their citizens are highly oppressed. The point being made is that for the country to be successful internationally, America still needs to be capitalist, while the population will not be allowed to reap the benefits of an open market like we do now. It just does not seem like a good idea to give up our pensions and 401k programs and only depend on an already wasteful spending government machine to invest our money instead.

Socialism in America cannot and will not work in our current structure, as I think far left Democrats are slowly finding out. Everyone having an equal opportunity in life is fine and dandy, but our country is not ready for a system that oppresses the middle class. It would be beneficial for American socialist leaders to come out of hiding and really map out what their agenda is, in full transparency. I think when Americans, left and right, really sit down and dissect the master plan, they will find that this system will eliminate 99 percent of the population from ever succeeding the success they have strived for years.

If any Americans are thinking maybe socialism might be a good idea for giving everyone equality and equity, please investigate the most efficient socialist nations and see how it is done and done correctly. We would need a heavy law enforcement presence, control of politicians government spending, a recycling of profit back to the citizens in some form, and a smaller population. The mass oppressive method AOC and "The Squad" are trying to accomplish, their objective will not work under the comparisons of the nations that are actually succeeding with socialism.

Addition to their failed plan of achieving leftist socialism, we should evaluate how the government relays messages to the people. If socialism is to work as it does in some Scandinavian countries, the government must be transparent. Biden partially ran his presidential campaign on being the most transparent president in history. Instead, we received confusion and misdirection. When the Afghanistan exit occurred, the Biden Administration avoided tough criticism and questions and instead utilized a psychological method for continually repeating that the situation was successful. The problem is, Americans love their soldiers, and Biden never took responsibility for their deaths as he should have.

Over the first year and a half of Biden's presidency, the administration, mainly through Press Secretary Jen Psaki, continually evaded and deflected questions and logical answers, nor did they admit their failures. This is what has caused such a drastic approval rating for Biden up until May of 2022, which, according to Quinnapiac, has Biden at 33 percent. A third of the country, which is almost half of Democrats, have decided Biden is not getting the job done. While Psaki is the peddler of lies and presidential cover up, one of the biggest problems is Department of Homeland Security Secretary Alejandro Mayorkas cannot answer any questions about anything Congress asks him on record. He claims he has "operational control" over the US/Mexican border. As we see the statistics continue to inflate, along with the video footage available for anyone to see, we know the border is a sieve of leaks, which I believe that is the one word we can use to describe the Biden Administration, leak.

Americans have no idea what the immigration plan is in the Biden Administration. All we can see are immigrants in mass crossing the Rio Grande and into the country illegally. It is becoming a traverse disaster, as immigrants are dying at the border by drowning, starvation, and other natural causes due to the treacherous journey to enter the country. This is also to go without saying the biggest risk they face is from the cartels that Biden has indirectly hired to be the nation's gatekeepers. Reports show you have to pay the cartel toll to even get close to the border at major entry points. I thought Texas US Congressman Chip Roy did a fantastic job of reflecting the State of Texas's frustration with Secretary Mayorkas during congressional questioning that took place the first week of May 2022. During that hearing on the border and the creation of the Disinformation Board with Mayorkas, the secretary had no tangible answers for the American people. As far as the border goes, he claims to have a plan, but he refuses to follow federal law of detaining immigrants while properly processing them. According to the Biden Administration's own report, too many immigrants are not being processed, detained, or vetted. As Secretary of the Department of Homeland Security, Mayorkas is not doing anything to secure this country. He is in fact a tyrant, and if a terrorist attack occurs on this nation that can be traced back to the giant welcome sign immigrants are chasing to enter this country at any costs, he should be held accountable under federal law. Currently, Mayorkas should resign immediately, if not, impeached to the fullest extent of our law process for his role in neglecting our border.

Of all the appointees in the Biden Administration, Mayorkas stood as someone that I would have thought to be more moderate or even Republican. After all, he is a Cuban immigrant that fled to the US after the Cuban Revolution. He later moved to California, which is likely where he became indoctrinated with liberalism, to attend UC-Berkeley. His family history is of fleeing oppressive regimes to greener pastures, as his mother fled Romania during WWII to Cuba and then fled Cuba for Florida in 1960 with her husband and young son, Alejandro. When we look at the family history, it appears evident that Mayorkas has a bias for immigration, which is likely why he embraced liberalism and keeps the border doors hanging wide open. What does not add up is to the comparisons of the radical left to Cuban government. I would think that Mayorkas would have not wanted to be part of an oppressive regime like Biden's, which his family would have run from also. After all, when the Cubans took to the streets in protest on July 11th, 2021, Biden didn't lift one finger to bring those refugees to this country. Had that been Mayorkas's family, they would have been left to the Cuban Government to do as they please.

As I have stated many times in this book already, and later, socialism is not set up to be fully functional in this country. We simply have too many people to properly fund every single American in a middle-class capacity. We need to keep fighting against this movement, though, as it appears progressives are not letting off the gas no matter how many times they fail.

CHAPTER 6
SOCIALISM FORWARD

So, let's say socialism is the future path American takes, or at least a watered-down version of it, what do we do as American citizens? Past socialist regimes have used authoritarian fear to keep the mass oppressed and hopeless. When people lose hope, your country loses their identity and ability to stand up for their beliefs. The short-lived Cuban uprising in 2021 proved that theory. Other socialist empires fared a bit better. Nazi Germany built a rabid killing machine based on the technological advancements paired with the promise of a utopian society. Sounds awfully familiar. The downfall of the Germans was simple: they fought too many enemies at once and did not have enough formidable allies. The Ally powers were too strong and united to destroy, especially when you divide your military front to try and invade a Russian people that have no quit in their DNA.

The Russian powerhouse, up until 1917, had a much different problem. They oppressed their people too much to where they had to die fighting or just simply die. The Romanovs had lost control of their own house, which leaked to the people throughout Russia and caused small uprisings all over the country. Eventually, the disturbances turned into larger riots, which eventually led to the overtaking and death of the Romanov royal dynasty. At that time in Russia, there were a lot of separate issues going on in the country which had the people severely divided. In the end, the Bolsheviks took power for some time and created a much stronger and more violent faction created by Vladimir Lenin.

When you take a deeper look at what the openly socialist politicians in Washington are saying in reference to Marxism, it really takes me back to Lenin's regime and his creation that let to Communism. It is absurd that we are in a country that allows such talk and these individuals to rise to power with the idea they can infiltrate our education system, our Congress, and even our White House. This should not be happening as the Fourteenth Amendment of the Constitution clearly states that, Article 1, "No state shall make or enforce any law which shall abridge the privileges or immunities of citizens of the United States; nor shall any State deprive any person of life, liberty, or property, without due process of law; nor deny to any person within its jurisdiction the equal protection of the laws." This is a powerful statement by our Founding Fathers as they set Americans up to own their own lives and property. Capitalism is a privilege that every single American in this country enjoys and uses to make their wealth. For House member Alexandria Ocasio-Cortez to continually come out and attack corporations that were created by American citizens that utilized capitalism for wealth is absolutely absurd. She is an active member of the far-left socialist movement headlined by Bernie Sanders and backlighted by George Soros. As Americans, we have far from received our due process for this administration to try and steal our rights under the Fourteenth Amendment.

What we are seeing in our own nation is a transfer over time to socialism. I believe their strategy hit warp speed when President Trump caused passionate division amongst the left and right wings. Left-wing socialists saw an opportunity to quickly implement their agenda as they held majority in every branch of government except the judiciary, which they may not need. In September and October of 2021, Nancy Pelosi pushed the House very hard to try and pass the socialism-created "reconciliation bill" that would cost taxpayers $3.5

trillion dollars. When you look at all the earmarks and pork barrels attached to this bill, it makes you wonder what all of the really would cost if they removed all of the fat. Yes, I think all republicans will agree that we need to improve the environment and be cleaner in our emissions; however, to bankrupt our nation to achieve it is not in the best interest of our government. It's even more disturbing to think that the US is the richest nation on the planet, and we are worrying about money. We dictate the world market, why are we having such a hard time balancing our spending? Our Congress's wasteful spending needs to come to an end. I'm only hopeful that President Biden's spend-trillions-of-dollars campaign does not create support for the economic crash we are facing.

On October 5th, 2021, Quinipiac University released their presidential approval rating report. Their results are astounding as only 38 percent of Americans support the administration. As a world leader, if your approval rating is that low, you should start changing course to keep your constituents happy. This is simple sociology: do what people want and they will be pleased. It doesn't always work that way in the real world, but when it comes to national interests, the masses do seem to have a better grasp as to what is hurting or helping their unique personal situations. When you leave Americans to die in a hostile, terrorist territory, increase taxes, push excessive spending, create inflation, look weak in international policy, push a socialist agenda that the whole country knows that's what it is, the American people will voice their opinions. It is amazing Jen Psaki can even walk anymore after holding on to the Biden Administration's lies and deception.

President Biden, always remember your history lessons from high school. When you have most of the country that is convicted and united on one single front, we are dangerous. This is the one simple reason America is and always be the greatest nation on this earth. A great president fought off the English empire with a group of angry farmers. The Brits offered President Washington the crown three times, and to their disappointment, he declined. A true American will not back down, we will not relinquish our free nation under democracy, we will not succumb to any threat, foreign or domestically infiltrated. We will weed out socialism and Marxists to restore our greatness in the world. You may think government is bigger than the opinions and expectations of the people, but don't forget your history. We are not in a second Civil War; we are in the second American Revolution, where the next George Washington will lead the people to victory.

The beginning of 2022 has been filled with many shootings and murders of police officers. We are seeing several democrats flip their stance on defunding the police, and in March of 2022, Biden released his plan to give a significant amount of funding to law enforcement. Mr. President, that seems a little too Republican of you. However, it makes me sick to hear these things happening that were the direct cause of liberal policy in large liberal city strongholds. I truly feel immense emotions for our law enforcement in every city as they are placed in a catch-22, damned if you do, damned if you don't. As a former law enforcement officer, I can understand how hard that decision is under distress. Socialist cowards such as DA Alvin Bragg in New York are allowing criminals to run free while awaiting trial for other crimes. This has turned into a disaster for Americans, as many cities are experiencing the same issues with the no-bail policy. Criminals are becoming more brazen. The West Coast is not much better as businesses are closing due to uncontested looting because bail reform doesn't punish offenders. The legal system is made up to redirect offenders, not reward offenders.

The last week of January brought a lot of emotions to the city of New York as Det. Jason Rivera was gunned down by an unknown assailant for no apparent reason, shortly after Officer Wilbert Mora was also murdered. It is a true American tragedy, but after seeing the Rivera funeral while watching Fox News, what I saw was a police show of force. The unity that those officers have in the city of New York is uncontested. It is a great agency with great officers that are being handcuffed by their own district attorneys. Fighting crime is very simple; Americans want to feel safe, and police officers keep us safe, so for the socialist movement to eliminate law enforcement is a bit off their agenda. It also does not make sense according to the leftist/socialist handbook. It would appear they should be spending more money on officers on the streets to utilize the Overton window theory, that more officers equal an almost military policing of citizens. I'd say Bernie's plan is not completely accurate.

Our socialists have the whole picture completely backwards. There is a huge aspect of creating a socialist society that far leaning liberals are completely dropping the ball on. When we reflect on the Det. Rivera's funeral procession, we see thousands of highly trained law enforcement officers in a committed show of force. These officers are great alphas in our country. We can say the same for our military troops. Most conservatives are gun-yielding, property-protecting, Constitutional, rough-and-tough alphas. If there is a successful socialist takeover, it would come from the right wing, not the left wing of our democracy in America.

As we look at other socialist/communists empires, they all have one thing in common: they utilized their countries' alphas to keep the order among the weaker thinking people. We have exerted this behavior as humans since the beginning of time. We stop bullying in our country in schools, which has been an issue since the schools started. The wolves will always eat the sheep, which I'm not saying bullying is acceptable, but it is in the cycle of life for all life forms. The main reason I personally never grasped the Democrats way of doing things is because everything they do is indirect and too sneaky for my taste. I know that if a Democrat is faced with extreme aggression, they will cower rather quickly. If my life is on the line, I would never trust a liberal to back me up. They don't appear to have loyalty to anything or anyone. They are absolutely the followers of our country to wannabe alphas like George Soros.

Adolf Hitler utilized a super-alpha soldier to nearly take over all of Europe. He did not take on a weaker, liberal ideology to create a united Germany versus the world mentality. The several Russian empires had the same objectives: take alphas and make the super soldiers, bigger bombs, bigger artillery, ruthless leadership. China is in the same category currently as they have strict laws against woke movements. China utilizes their weak in weak positions and emblazons their alpha into military, sportsman, and political glory.

The faulty plan in the US socialist movement is when you look at their structure, there is a head figure(s) that is out of the spotlight which is a "bully," he, she, they, instill their agenda. The left politicians take that agenda and follow the playbook given to them by the wannabe alpha(s). With the left being complete followers of the powerful, they utilize the only group of alphas they can, minority groups. Some right-wing supporters can consider ANTIFA as part of that group, but I don't consider anyone that wears a mask to commit crimes against other humans and businesses as alphas. ANTIFA preys on the weak, which in turn makes them cowards.

When assessing minority groups in the US, you can clearly see how the leftist utilize a very emotional African American community to achieve their agenda. The democrats are the ultimate gaslighters to this ethnic group. Throughout the history of our country, white Americans have enslaved African Americans in one way or another. Slavery still exists for them in the present, just in a different, less brutal way, Democrat puppeteering. Today, it appears that African Americans have ample opportunity, which they do; however, political circles have learned to enslave them in another way, in a socioeconomic angle. Minority groups are being controlled by the weak puppet masters in Washington. The growing error in this objective is that African Americans are now more educated than ever before, they are more free thinking than ever. This ethnic group is turning their history around to no longer be looked at as a minority group, but rather an equal to all. It is a great feat that is well deserved. The last task of their freedom that they need to grasp is their freedom from political sway.

In April of 2020, I moved to Atlanta, Georgia, from rural Ohio for a job opportunity and found that what I thought about minority oppression is not quite true. One of the first statements from an African American businessman I encountered, who is now a great friend, was, "Welcome to Black Mecca." I thought about that statement for a solid year, while observing what is going on around me in this huge city. My findings were very simple: Atlanta has great financial and education opportunities for minority growth. It is a great city for equality, just as what I think Dr. Martin Luther King would be extremely proud of.

The significance of African American minority success is important in the grand scheme of liberal socialist takeovers. Leaders have misjudged the desperation of the African American community. They no longer need white liberal bureaucrats to succeed. In fact, I see more and more minorities on both CNN and Fox News. I do believe as more and more minorities become educated, there will be a leveling out of those demographics among political parties.

As democrat minority voters swing more and more moderate to independent, they lose their ability to transition into their full socialist government. So, my friends of many national origins, the government needs you, you don't need them. Have your control over your people and demand that our at-risk communities and schools be addressed. This failure of many administrations does not need to happen. Find your positive leaders and encourage them to rise with the intention of politicking more improvement. Candace Owens preaches family structure among the black communities as the key to improving the quality of life, and I do believe she is right. I see this as a positive in the area of Atlanta that I live in. We have many families of all ethnic groups that are either intact or separated families with both parents very much involved in the progress of their children, which generates success in my community. As Americans, we must acknowledge that the family structure is a key element to lower crime rates in at-risk communities.

The solution is not as difficult as the endless politicians of the past and present would suggest. If any administration would have put the funds aside to really make a difference, common citizens would not be faced with such obstacles that appear to be unheard of by our elected officials. At-risk communities are more than just a talking point to earn votes. In the future we need to empower these ethnic groups to see all sides of the spectrum before the next political candidate shows up with their never-ending broken promises that they never intend on fulfilling or fall just short of a good faith effort.

Continuing with minority adjustments, I found myself remembering a required reading of a book when I worked at a juvenile treatment facility for high at-risk youth. *Healing Racism in America*, by Nathan Rutstein, continued to explore his personal stories or racism and how to solve it in order to unify humankind in peace. In chapter two, "Separate but Equal," he states, "Not even through the American Civil War, in which six hundred thousand men were killed in a struggle over slavery, was racism eradicated. The Civil Rights Movement, they point out, with all of its fury and high expectations, also failed to solve the core problem." In two big equal rights events in American history, not one piece of legislation came about. Moving forward, I do believe that we create a much harsher law regarding racism. In our country, we just cannot tolerate it in the last few areas where it is abundant. Legislation needs to be made that makes racist remarks from anyone of any color a misdemeanor. Upon prosecution, that individual would have to attend a healing racism course to satisfy the courts. It is a small system to boot; however, I believe in an overall understanding of how each ethnic group works. The fact is that people of every race have their own set of issues and happiness. If Americans do not take the time to appreciate each other with love and understanding, we will keep moving in reverse.

Even today, with all the BLM movements, along with other civil rights groups pushing for legislation, nothing happened. Instead, the message became corrupted by greed and infiltrated by Marxism. At the end of the day, the aftermath of the George Floyd shooting amounted to nothing. It is also true to note that while leaders in Washington, DC, stood proud in front of the TV cameras to support anti-police agendas, they did nothing in Congress. It is a true travesty that minority communities are always led down this path to empty promises. The two-hundred-year-old trend needs to end, and that can occur only by intelligent vote, regardless of party lines. Until the government starts dumping millions of dollars into at-risk communities, along with the upgrading of the school systems in those communities, there will never be a positive change.

History only repeats itself if we keep allowing it to do so. At no time in history has a socialist society allowed for equality of other races. What we are being fed by progressive Democrats are simply a lie. It will be much of the same except the segregation will be non-racial but instead strictly by monetary class. Progressives want nothing more than to sit on their elite thrones and watch the peasants slave away at the dirty work. In my world, there would be balance, except there would be a strong middle class and formidable upper-class, while my system will elevate much of the lower class through education, opportunity, strong religious beliefs, and strengthening the morality of family structure. The racist circle of failure will continue until someone dares to jump out of it.

When Democrats push to raise corporate taxes, it made me wonder why they would want to do that when some of their colleagues are in that tax bracket. The answer came to me in a press release announcing Elon Musk became majority shareholder of Twitter. I imagine former CEO Jack Dorsey is likely taking a double dose of anxiety meds right about now. I feel that most Americans are not in the loop with Musk and his agendas. He is by far the wealthiest individual on the planet, which means there is very little any government can do to control his ability to influence whatever he wants. With Twitter being a censorship tool for progressives, Musk will step into that board of directors and likely make some huge changes to the functionality of the popular social media site. I would be willing to bet extensive changes are on the rise. Musk has stepped out to the forefront and inserted himself smack dab in the middle of this civil war. Note how many Republicans mention his efforts on their behalf, which is very little. I think even Republicans are hesitant to jump on the bandwagon because no one really knows the guy, or his principles. From where I stand, he is the only American with influence to take on anyone and everyone at any given time. I applaud his courage and vision for a better and balanced future America. Only time will tell if Musk can withstand the barrage that will surely come from leftists.

Corporate America will do what they always do when Democrats are in office: they will shop the world for the best tax rate and move their companies overseas. This method historically creates less jobs, which makes the job market more competitive, which will suppress the lower class as they are the ones lacking the skills to obtain the upper-echelon jobs that will improve the quality of living. Instead, it makes the government address the growing unemployment problem by expanding the welfare system that causes working class citizens to fund. The Democrat system for corporate America is a forever flawed system that fails every single presidential cycle. I'm not saying the Republicans get it right all the time, but they are closer to successful.

The answer to their methods is not clearly stated truthfully; however, Democrats are always on their soap box trying to rally the low-income people to be upset with corporations for getting good tax breaks. What I feel they are doing is masking the excuse for the government to take more in taxes so they have more capitol to spend on free programs that will make everyone dependent on the government, which is socialism. Big money theft from corporations equals big government.

Even though the US is already a semi-socialist nation, we still must stay competitive in the world market, so for members of "The

Squad" and Bernie Sanders to always speak about doing away with capitalism is an absolute farse. Every nation on the planet participates in a capitalist global market. It is the only way to keep your country afloat with imports and exports. Their goal is to turn the people against capitalism in order to allow for big government and special interests groups to keep the wealth for the 1 percent. No economy will become prosperous without international trade.

Without corporate tax breaks, it is very likely, as history suggests, that corporations will shop other competitive markets overseas or south of the American border. As Democrats and far left figures push for a near twenty dollars an hour minimum wage, this will spike inflation further, as companies will have to raise the price of their goods to pay for the now more expensive work force. Throw the new tax rate on top of the higher wages and company profit margins are going to take a hit. This formula could be the downfall of many companies that are already struggling to keep their doors open.

The company I manage has much of the same issue. With Atlanta being a highly liberal city, leaders have urged businesses to raise their wages by nearly double. For our company to stay competitive with semi-skilled workers, we have had to adjust our pay scale to accommodate the common worker, which has obtained negotiation power during the Biden Administration. Luckily, our ownership, sales team, and management predicted this wage spike, and we were able to get ahead of it. We will survive it; however, there are a lot of companies that are not going to be able to staff their business do to workforce affordability. As Biden continues to suggest the government spend their ghost money, the prospect of another strong inflation spike cold occur.

Socialism forward, according to extreme left-wing individuals, appears to be a chaotic mess of anti-everything, cancellation, violating our rights to happiness and a destruction of our borders and economy. Decades down the road, Joe Biden will go down as the single worst president in the history of this country. Regardless of the constant disasters Biden continues to manifest, I believe the next president will, in fact, must fix these issues. The border can be solidified, international respect and leadership can be restored, the economy can balance out. I have doubts, however, that America can go back to the solid democracy we were created for, but I do believe we can still work to protect American rights under the Constitution. It will take a strong leader that has to emerge in time for 2024. I voted for Trump and supported his policies, but I do not think he is the exact savior of our nation. He has built a very solid foundation that I truly believe half of the nation can grow on as democratic patriots. We must continue to go against the grain when it comes to left-wing socialists. Their methods are highly oppressive to all Americans and will create a 1 percent oligarchy in this country. We cannot become a nation of elitists, while the rest of us are just ants in the ant farm.

We must decide, as Americans, if we want to continue forward with the re-revolution of democracy. The national stage is set-up to allow for this battle of old-world democracy and new-age left socialism. I firmly believe that if this war continues, this country is doomed and will regress, while several developing nations with alternative motives for the world will emerge to take our place as rule enforcers. The alternative is a compromise where there is a semi-socialist nation where individual prosperity can occur while capping the income of major corporations without giving the government too much power as a profit sharing with the people will keep the economy moving forward.

CHAPTER 7

THE PLAN

The demo-socialist party is in full steam and appears to not be in a hurry to slow down before the 2022 primary, where, if democracy holds true, they will likely lose their power hold on all branches of our government. George Soros-backed Bernie Sanders still sits high on his communist throne and holds the moderate democrats hostage with the power he and his band of socialist flunkies have over Nancy Pelosi. No deal in Congress will be completed until Bernie says so. Mark Levin said on *Life, Liberty and Levin,* which airs on Fox News, that the socialists in Congress promote such a negative movement and no one looks like they are happy. I thought long and hard about that statement, and it is very evident that statement to be true, and it posed a question; if we are going down the socialist rabbit hole, why does it have to be this way that is proposed by George Soros?

I have a proposition for a different socialist regime, my way. It is obvious that the current plan is to take everything they can away from the people in order to have the general public begging for government assistance. Freedom of speech was the first to go. We are constantly edited and critiqued to the point its counterproductive to talk. Cancel culture from big tech is out of control. They have basically bullied their way into a government-contracted audit company that is severely one sided. This is a very Hitleresque method of doing things.

What they are trying to do is keep anyone else outside of their bubble of trusted confidants to rise to power. It's oppressive.

I understand the method, but why do we have to oppress to create the agenda? In my socialism plan, you don't have to. If the goal is to limit wealth, which in turn limits power, I will propose a five-hundred-million-dollar salary cap on Corporate America. Anything more will go in a government-watched trust fund that my signature will be the only requirement to release to the general public. This revenue will be sent out equally to every American as a bonus stipend that is distributed monthly. It is not a good thing to weaken our economy with less-than-stellar product. We need to keep that high standard that will attract buyers from around the world as we do now. The salary cap allows for companies such as Microsoft and Facebook from becoming more powerful than the federal government, which creates a power struggle and sense of untouchability for such individuals as Jeff Bezos, Mark Zuckerberg, Bill Gates, and George Soros, just to name a few. Instead of eliminating the middle class and moving people to the lower level of poverty as what the current socialist regime asserts, I will eliminate the lower class and migrate them into the middle class by distributing profits. There is only one catch to receiving this stipend: you must be at work 95 percent of the days your scheduled. On the tax side, the government will still need to collect taxes, but I will set that tax rate every two years based upon the market trends. This number will likely be around 20–25 percent payroll tax.

One of my favorite topics to talk about is defunding the police. In any world, socialist, democratic, monarchy, communist, this is never a situation that will ever work. We live in a world of mental illness everywhere. You cannot curb every single crime by continually turning your back on law enforcement. The statistics for rising crime in cities that have cut law enforcement funding are astronomical. We must have law and order. We have a drug epidemic that doesn't seem to matter anymore in the Biden Administration, hence the open-door policy that he has allowed. This is likely far off base, but you'd think the cartels are in the Biden's pocket. I believe that the American Justice System has just about attempted every angle for judicial reform.

It would be a great idea to look at the countries globally that are succeeding in the fight against crime. According to worldpopulationreview.com, Iceland has the lowest crime rate in the world. When looking into how Iceland created a safe environment for their people, we must understand that the entire country's population is around 340,000. However, their methods are extremely effective and can be utilized in mass magnitude in our country. They are our socioeconomic experiment. All we must do is follow and advance their outline. What Iceland suggests is that we look at our equality in a deep perspective. They have a zero-tolerance policy for inequality. What our socialist counterparts are suggesting is to take a semi-false pretense of oppression away from minorities and transform it into white rage. Folks, this is not going to work. Yes, American Europeans have been-less-than stellar in their use of other races here in American. I highly admire those affected but have yet overcome it. I root for that type of person, but to reverse it back to create a power push to attach to middle-class whites is going to create even more divisive behavior. The plan is to wipe the slate clean. Everyone accepts their responsibility and moves on to equality. No exceptions. Every genre of humanity will be accepted equally; gays, transgenders, Christians, atheists, white, black, etc. will all be equal in my country. I will create tougher laws on oppressive behavior.

We cannot abolish the law enforcement, but we will retrain them to be community-based peace officers (not in the way progressives define it). As a country, we need to appreciate the great police that we do have, and the ones that abuse their power will be dealt with harshly and swiftly. I will spend government funds to train law enforcement personnel to act appropriately towards every ethnicity with respect until it is apparent kindness will not work anymore. We will not tolerate violent crime, sentences for repeat offenders will be even more harsh. My officers will heavily patrol at-risk areas until they are no longer considered at-risk. We will create safe neighborhoods where children can walk the streets again without fear. My government will cut funding towards the trillions of wasteful dollars the socialists want to spend and dump it into at-risk, high-crime areas to build better schools and vocational facilities. We will fund minority colleges and allow hands-on case work with all peoples of color in at-risk area. Children will no longer starve or become lost on their path towards greatness. We will educate all children in the schools to be great human beings, not only to yourself but to your future children and spouses. If we preach family unity while providing programming that will encourage this type of family approach, there will be a higher likelihood of keeping a child out of the system. Poverty will decline as we save the family structure our current and past administrations have led us to abandon.

The American justice system needs a complete overhaul. We can still be tough on major crimes while still giving offenders the opportunity of redemption. I don't really think most crimes have an unfair sentencing and ability to be released judicially early, so fixing that part of the legal process is not as necessary. I would like to implement a point system for offenses of all levels. I believe that recidivism can be deterred with eliminating the mantra that comes with having a felony label. There's no hope for someone after the are labeled a felon. Having a ten-point system that will allow offenders to lower their threat level will give all offenders the ability to take your record away after a period of time as a lawful citizen.

Our border will be secured at all costs. Unidentified migrants will not be accepted, and in order to enter this country you will have to apply for entrance through the DHS. This will start a series of background inquiries that will assure this great nation that we are only bringing in migrants of solid moral structure. We are fighting crime, not inviting it in. It is absolutely appalling that President Biden has not moral compass for our national security at the border. There are too many criminals coming through along with major cartel members and peoples with ill intentions from countries that are not so friendly with us. This will stop under my watch.

The socialist agenda for immigration is a false pretense. It does not make sense to allow undocumented immigrants into our country without being vetted and vaccinated. It is obvious what is really going on, as the democrats are playing superhero to the migrants yet allowing them to be treated inhumanely at the border until they are dumped off into some random city. The end agenda that they somehow think is going to work is they will flood the country at any cost with migrants that they feel will further their stronghold in Washington. The faulty plan is not going to work because those people still fled oppression and are walking into another country headed in that same direction. These targeted individuals entering the country are not going to vote for any socialist regime. I find it extremely odd that when the caravan of Hatians that were escaping their own dictator-backed government overthrow, President Biden wanted to send all of the back to Haiti. Having migrants fleeing oppressive regimes does not fit the Biden Administration agenda, so off you go. However, news coverage was quick to pick up the mass exodus of migrants in Del Rio, Texas, that Biden had to salvage what he could of the situation, and virtually overnight, all the migrants disappeared from the encampment, most likely placed on busses and shipped all over the country. The same also applies to the spring uprising in Cuba. Cubans demanded they be given their freedom by the Cuban Government and were attacked for protesting. Cuban citizens in their country along with the thousands of Cubans in Florida pleaded and protested for President Biden to intervene to save the oppressed. Our president did what he does best, turn his back on people in need.

Under my control, the US will never cower, we will never falter. When people from other nations cry out for help, we will answer. When our own people cry out for help, we will answer. Kamala Harris is so out of touch with the border crisis, which has the simplest of answers, finish Trump's plan, that it is a disgrace to even have her presence there anymore at all. The border will be secure. We will find out who everyone that wants to enter are and document them. We will finish building the great wall Trump started. We will support the Border Patrol and their efforts to protect this great nation. President Biden, problem solved.

Gun violence is rapidly becoming an out-of-control problem in most metro areas. In democrat-run cities, violent crimes are at all-time highs. The problem is at-risk areas. In some cities, those neighborhoods are so dangerous, law enforcement do not show up until the gunfire stops. As a nation, our government has done absolutely nothing to curtail this horrendous trend. We have a vice president that bails out felons that are at high risk for recidivism, and in one case, a Kamala Harris bail recipient murdered another citizen with a firearm in a road rage incident months after being bailed out in Minnesota. Biden also refuses to acknowledge the civil war going on in Portland, Oregon. People, there is a violent situation that is a year ongoing that no left-wing politician will even look at. Business are being looted and burnt to the ground still. Violent crime is up and no one on the left is doing anything to stop it. President Trump tried to intervene in Portland in 2019 by suggesting help from the National Guard, but Portland Mayor Ted Wheeler refused and stated the state police would handle it. What did our great city leaders do? They voted to take away fifteen million dollars from the police budget. In the meantime, officers retired in mass; they quit or transferred to other jurisdictions. Since the defund, violence continued to rise, and the city looks like Mogadishu at night (God forbid left-wing idiot millennials get up early and go to a job, instead of sleeping all day and rioting all night).

Democratic cities are starting to backpedal on the Defund the Police movement due to voter unfavourability polling. Even democrats want to feel safe in their city. In the city of Atlanta, it is my dually isolated opinion that Mayor Keisha Lance Bottoms ceased to seek another term as mayor due to the city's unified opinion that she failed as mayor to properly address the rising violent crime trend in the city. Even the prestigious suburb of Buckhead, inside the north end of the perimeter, pushed around the idea of secession from the city of Atlanta and creating their own municipality, which would be self-funded. Their agenda of taking away the only boundary of safety in this country is going to cost the city of Atlanta millions of dollars in tax revenue that they depend on to properly fun the city. I'm sure if we were to look at several other major cities in the US we would find other high-tax-revenue areas that are seeking options to keep their strategically planned business centers safe from violent crime.

One aspect of our country that the current administration blatantly ignores is our ability to take advantage of our resources. Look at our supply situation that is occurring at nearly every port entry designation on our coasts. If we have a driver shortage that the administration suggests, then we need to utilize our federal resources. We have a very well-equipped and efficient National Guard that is ready and willing to help Americans. Biden was asked about deploying National Guard for this very purpose by a media outlet, and he seemed to like the notion but later backtracked via lie whiteout Press Secretary Jen Psaki. It would have been a very effective option and a positive mark for Biden to show the American people that he is trying to help. Instead, he chose to follow the George Soros/Bernie Sanders' socialist agenda to fully submerge the country into oblivion. As future socialist king of America, I would have pulled all the strings I could to provide goods that my people need and deserve as the greatest nation on the planet. It's absurd that normal human beings can think the way puppet Biden is thinking.

Our government structure in democracy has failed. In fact, the negligent patterns of our congressmen and women have persistently over time grown out of control with their wasteful spending and pork barrels and earmarks that they trick Americans with their sickening bills they pass without regard of what their people truly want. In my forty years on this planet, not one politician has ever called, emailed, or mailed me anything asking me what I want out of them. This is true all the way from president of the United States to school board members. The reason I have not ever been polled is because they know myself and many other Americans can stand on our own two feet against them. For example, I don't want my tax money paying for a fence that protects President Biden's beach house in Delaware. I want him to build a fence around our southern border. I also don't want my money spent on free childcare and free housing for felons. I don't want my police defunded.

Congress has to be abolished. Once democracy officially falls and I take over, I will dismiss all members of Congress and reevaluate the potential candidates for my Parliament. I will assemble sections based on expertise of the individuals and need of the country. We don't want failed career politicians such as Pete Buttigieg running the Department of Transportation when he was an absolute disaster as mayor of South Bend, Indiana. I will put together a team of transportation experts to head that office of my Parliament. I will take the brightest military leaders that understand how to extract Americans first from torn nations and bring the home. In fact, my leaders would not have lost Afghanistan. We would have wiped out every terrorist in that country and developed a formidable military base there indefinitely. I will assemble the greatest financial minds in the country to keep our economy filled with fresh ideas that make our nation wealthy without creating money out of thin air. We will control the world market with strategy and quality import and export. I will put together the best international policymakers to govern the world when disagreements occur. We will be the judge, jury, and executioner of the world. Europe will act as our little brothers again and fall in line with the American Agenda. My cabinet will be filled with advisors that are true American Patriots, and I will screen their merits myself to assure they are of solid red, white, and blue heart. Our flag will have massive respect in every inch of this world. I will not put up with war lords that massacre their people such as China.

I will not allow China to run this world or have a voice in power. They will be knocked back where they belong. I will not allow China to strategically maneuver their forces all around America. They are currently in place to attack the great soil of the US, and President Biden is too worried about spending 3.5 trillion dollars on nothing instead of noticing the threat to this country.

The US will rekindle our love of our past, ancestors, and Founding Fathers. This is the only way we can sway our past failures. After sitting down to help my son write a research paper about the Great Depression, the history book cited Herbert Hoover's government handouts as the reason as to why the stock market crashed. That bit of history reminds me of what the Biden Administration is doing with our failing economy. Free handouts and printing more money than what we have in reserve equals a failed economy. It appears that we have not been taking the time to take those failures from the past and applying them to current situations to prevent the same mistakes repeatedly. We need to end that as Americans. We will keep that history, good and bad, and take the lessons from them so we do not continue repeating history. It is very astounding as to why all the intelligent people with their political science degrees have not figured out how to keep our country moving forward by not continuing the cycle of failure.

It is impeccable that Americans start to hold our heads high again. We are America and bow to no other nation. That pride is going to come back, and our nationalism is going to prosper. The people are going to find their pride, and that is first done by having a leader they can trust and takes care of the needs of all Americans. As the leader of the country, I will look after all our people. We will be tough on crime and sympathetic to victims of crime. America will have renewed faith in our law enforcement system, while creating a system to reassess criminals in an attempt to rehabilitate every offender. More programming will be available, while the advanced criminals will be subject to further direction to help find their hope in their field of interest.

I cannot talk enough about our military reputation pre-1991 Gulf War compared to current military downfalls. The American military used to be full of warriors that successfully completed missions all over the world. Today, most Americans view our military as soft and underprepared, due to faulty leadership. I, too, believe that assessment to be true. In my military, we will build warriors again. America will be so advanced technologically that China will stop pursuing our greatness and Russia will go back into to silent hiding. Our Special Forces will again be truly special. We will be so elite that every nation will look at us as mythological. When you look up the top ten special forces in the world, only the US will show up on YouTube.

US generals have lost their ability to lead, so I will sift through our ranks for the brightest and best that the world has. It sickens me to see General Milley and Joint Chief of Staff Austin on TV spewing deniability and deflecting responsibility to their failures. We are the biggest and the best, we should not have strategic failures out of our military leaders. It is unacceptable, although I do understand that people do make mistakes, but to have the military disaster that has unfolded in the last twenty years is inexcusable. Everyone currently with a star on they lapel will be removed and replaced with generals that will get the job done with perfection. Citizens of the US should be able to count on the military to successfully defend this nation and the nations of those that cannot defend themselves. The "we did our best" answer is no longer acceptable.

Weakness will be eliminated from our troops thought process. Currently, the White House is putting guys like John Kirby on TV, crying while reading a speech to President Putin! I'd be willing to be that every media outlet in Russia has John Kirby on a loop crying as we look like a bunch of soft crybabies. That is not the American way. It is valid to point out that George Washington did not cry when England occupied the US. Instead, he put his boy pants on and crossed the Delaware River and destroyed out oppressors. To me, our leadership acts like a bunch of kindergarten teachers.

I will also neutralize the longest running war on the planet. Israel and the Palestinians have been at war for thousands of years. Does anyone think that may be a little too long? What I propose is a forced truce that will last a lifetime. The US will occupy the disputed areas with our own troops and declare all areas of Israel are for all people. We will police the country heavily, and if the violence continues, we will permanently occupy Israel as a territory of the US. Enough is enough. I stand with Israel, but global peace supersedes any relationship the US may have. It is my firm strategic belief that when the US is a large presence in the Middle East, there seems to be more cooperation by the nations in the region. I feel this would be true if the US had boots on the ground promoting peace throughout Israel. I do not believe Hamas or any other faction in that area of the world would strike the US, while we know Israel will not as well. The fact remains that Israel is treated much like Ukraine. Everyone knows there's a problem, but no one wants to really get involved to solve it.

War-torn areas are a major problem; however, if peaceful allies band together in truthful good faith, a lot of reconciliation can be achieved. The times of warlords will be over. In my America, we will not stand for Chinese Uyghur genocide is completely unacceptable, and my country will invoke an embargo of all Chinese goods into and out of the country. I will not stand by and fund a nation that murders their own people. When it comes to China, I stand with great leaders like Enes Freedom (Kanter) in his movement to end genocide and reveal our hypocrisies when it comes to China. No country on the planet is holding China accountable for any action that is against society norms. China could invade Taiwan tomorrow and massacre the entire island and no one would blink an eye for the Taiwanese people. Our government is full of hypocrites that need to be exposed and excused. I have no room for cowardice fake leaders that will not utilize the power of America to stand on their own two feet. It's like a paramedic showing up at a scene with a patient choking to death and the paramedic just stands there and does nothing. It is neglectful, and with the current administration running the show, consider your country on their own and left for dead. Biden does not have the backbone to go against his special interest groups.

It is an obvious assessment that when you watch a G20 summit or other world gathering of leaders, every national leader does not make a move without the blessing of the US. This statement held true until Biden became president. If Americans would get their heads out of the fabricated liberal cheerleading media and pay attention to what the world news are saying about our country and current leadership, you will see that we are the punchline of every joke across the world. I don't really care if every country deep down hates the US; however, the problem persists; the world has no solid leader if the US leadership is weak. There is not one person in Europe who is willing to rise to the occasion to lead the world in morality and justice against China, Russia, or any other nation that potentially would pose a threat to mankind. In my opinion, one international strategy Trump made highly successful was his ability to sit down and meet with every negative world power and let them know face to face what the position of the United States would be about how they conduct themselves. The world became very stable under Trump out of fear for the big stick the US possesses and threatened to use if anyone stepped out of line. Even Putin held back from initiating any kind of hostility towards anyone.

It became very evident of Trump's successful international policy by seeing how China completely backed down from Trump in the trade war between the two nations. In the past, there were "norms" when it came to international trade with China. When Trump showed up, he realized the benefits of dealing with China in the past had a one-sided benefit that America did not profiteer from. Although Trump backed away from direct involvement in negotiations with China, he did place the right people in place to keep the momentum going while the president shifted his focus to domestic issues. In short, Trump's Administration spent a good part of its tenure countering

China's world dominance push, and had this not happened, China would have advanced a very dangerous agenda that they are now initiating on a sleeping Biden Administration.

Where Trump was strong, Biden flipped it to be weak. America went from world neutralizer to world walk-over, just as when Obama was president. The difference now is Biden is becoming more and more left and lacking competence. Obama was still sharp and had a visual boundary. I don't think Biden knows where boundaries are anymore. If he does still have cognitive strategic decision-making abilities, the country is in worse shape than I initially thought. The left may be able to trick vulnerable Americans that we need to be reactive traffic cops, but the world sees us as the apex of society, and we lost world leadership the day Biden took office. In my administration, I will take back world power by being firm and knowing my enemy very well. This method worked very well for Trump, and it would work again.

In my administration, I would greatly research historically what worked with moderation when it comes to negotiation of both parties. There are policies that we can gel together from the past with a few tweaks to update into modern methods of government. We are currently outdated in our ways of governing, while always trying to reinvent policies that have never been successful not only in US history but also world history. There is no reason to have a political civil war over far-right and far-left policies. As Americans, we can negotiate to a moderate way of living together in harmony. The initial design of this great nation was intended to bring people from all walks of life together in one unit of strength, where every type of person brings their own specialty to humanity. This is the very thought process I possess and how I see every American in this country. The divisiveness going on today is no longer acceptable. Moderation and the true definition of human equity and equality are the goals. We can no longer take the strategic wordplay of today's major media outlets that are designed to keep us always picking a side. This country is not meant to have a He-Man versus Skeletor methodology. We are the keepers of the big stick among all nations of the world, and we can only swing it with effectiveness if we unite as one people.

CHAPTER 8

GET READY

While reading this chapter, keep in mind that a future socialist take-over by any side is not what this country needs, nor am I suggesting that I would lead an insurrection against the United States of America's government. The statements that follow are merely hypothetical rhetoric to give readers a realistic view of how patriotic Americans that value Democracy over life will likely react. The socialist agenda I propose is not a total farse, as many of my methods are already in use by several socialist nations, such as Norway and Iceland. In retrospect, if a total socialist takeover were to happen, which included the deliberate dismantling of any or all Amendments of the United States Constitution, I would expect much of what I describe in the following passages to occur.

America is in a very dire situation that is going to take careful maneuverability on both sides of the aisle to figure out how to positively move forward; however, there is nothing on this planet that can break the true American spirit. This country is still the land of dreams and prosperity. It's the land of new starts and universal love for people of all forms, races, sexes, and religions. Our ancestors may have made drastic mistakes, but we have always overcome them and built our nation stronger than the generation before. A president that is a treasonous tyrant will not change that. We will prevail stronger than we were before.

Look at what radical socialism is, a group of weak people that cannot stand on their own two feet and have to weaponize the government to oppress the strong, faithful Americans that are the heart of the country by putting a financial squeeze on them. They target the youth in the education system, propagate their agenda with a promise of a utopian society. Our public schools are littered with the trick of Critical Race Theory, which is a system of creating racism to combat racism in our schools. How does that make any sense? CRT is the start of the socialist agenda. As digital schooling during the pandemic became a huge inconvenience in my home, it did bring to light how our curriculum is created to shame anyone that is anti-socialism.

I would say that we need to take bold action to place the emphasis of education and revert it back to higher learning education in order to improve our national educational standing. What has begun to happen are the parents of these students have already started the movement with good grace. Parents that pay the local taxes to fund the paychecks of these teachers and administrators need to keep having their voices heard. These hateful methods of educating students to hate one another for atrocities that their ancestors may or may not have been involved in is an absurd theory to attempt to implement. The focus needs to be on higher education and international accelerated academic advancement.

The Organization for Economic Cooperation and Development (OECD) submits many nations to participate in an assessment test (PISA) that covers science, reading, and mathematics for secondary education-aged students in order to evaluate where each nation ranks internationally. When I viewed the results of the overall compilation from the last evaluation in 2018, I found it unacceptable and absurd that the overall ranking of the United States education system ranks twenty-second in the world behind (in order from first to twenty-second) China, Singapore, Estonia, Japan, South Korea, Canada, Finland, Poland, Ireland, United Kingdom, Slovenia, New Zealand, Sweden, Netherlands, Denmark, Germany, Belgium, Australia, Switzerland, Norway, and the Czech Republic. Being second on this list in unacceptable, and I am willing to bet when the tests are calculated later this year as OECD states the US will move a little further down the rankings. Once upon a time, the US would strive to be the best of the best. It seems, today, we are so consumed with social acceptability that we have forgotten how to be academically competitive. It is also relevant to not that while China is catching up with us in military dominance and international trading, they are also the top nation according to OECD's PISA assessment.

Aside from woke policies, one other major problem with our educational system is the Teachers Unions. One of the biggest educational failures in modern time is American Federation of Teachers president Randi Weingarten. With the world ranking of twenty-second, Weingarten has failed the millions of students and parents in this country, as our country should have a much higher bar for teaching our nation's youth. Instead, she spends her time pushing liberal agendas and trying to keep teachers from returning to the classroom during and after the biggest waves of the pandemic. She has encouraged educators to become lazy, which will soon be proven to reflect on our status in the international education community. The fact that we can see Weingarten spouting hatred towards parents on social media and news outlets, rather than hearing Secretary of Education Miguel Cardona's plan to put us back on the map as an education powerhouse, says a lot about who is really running our education system.

Cardona and Biden need to push aside the bureaucracies and make education a priority for this country. Instead of giving the Ukraine billions in funds to fight a war that we are now funding, put that money into our education system. There needs to be a purge of all teachers that support woke policies and far-left liberalism and bring in educators that do not have a political agenda. These children need to have their minds filled with the information and training that will allow them to be successful in their future endeavors. These kids need to be groomed for future positive leadership from high school all the way into college.

Our universities are a problematic disaster that became initiated from the seeds planted at the high school levels. If the 2022 election does not flip the power back to a balanced ideology and the radical left is able to fulfill their master plan, there will be a chain of events that follow in our educational system. The colleges are an exact example of how inferior-minded people are using their positions of power to infiltrate and use the alpha students in the world. The good thing about that strategy is most alphas are such good leaders they refuse to follow a method they deem weak. However, the alphas are not the target group, the millennial college students that have no political affiliation yet are prime for manipulation are. They take these students and implant socialist ideology right off the bat. I ask any college student, past, present, and future, to really see everything you are taught from several different angles. There are a hundred million Americans that are saying you are being taught incorrectly through a dangerous manipulation of your eager mind. Do not cave right away to the liberal-communist theories that are thrown in your face. Under my tenure in power, the education system from preschool to doctorate will be rebranded to accept only the highest standards, which will jump our great nation to the top of the education standings across the globe. We cannot advance as a society without being the best in the classroom.

After the education system is tainted, the socialists will attack the severe threat groups to their plan. The first thing they will do is round up all the resistant Republican leaders and remove them from office. The ones that resist will be imprisoned. When this happens, rural America will start to assemble their masses without much detection. Crime deterrent agencies will then be dismissed from duty and a carefully selected military presence will be deployed, likely NATO troops, to maintain order. This will buy time for the right to get organized due to the chaos in the large cities, as metro areas will be a free for all. Once order in cities is restored, they will round up all felons and put them in large concentration camps and likely be left there for an unregulated amount of time. Keep in mind, the US Constitution will not be in effect anymore. socialist leaders will develop their own documentation that all Americans will have to submit to.

Since the Second Amendment is no longer valid, the false government will send a gestapo out to round up all the guns in the nation. Resistance will be dealt with harshly, and many people will be killed. When notice of all firearms are to be collected is issued across the nation, the revolution will begin. This is the point where I will rise to rally the great American people to defeat another foreign invader from our country.

At this moment, rural America will take arms with the many militias that are sworn to protect the Constitution. Former police officers and discharged or retired military personnel will take lead on organizing the onslaught eradication of socialist from our country. A list of known socialists will be distributed, and they will be hunted and apprehended for trial. Once leadership is apprehended, NATO will no longer have the jurisdictional authority to fire one bullet on anyone in the US, just as what happened with the Taliban. Secret Service will be asked to surrender to the new American regime and be instantly deputized to apprehend whomever the socialists deem is the leader of the country along with anyone that sympathizes with that said leader. Most likely, Joe Biden will be replaced with the person who has been pulling all the strings behind the scenes, so a quick apprehension of the next individual will have to happen.

It is my strong opinion, based on my own personal interactions with socialists, they are weak by themselves and will be relatively easy to conquer. When you have a regime change, the alphas will emerge and take what they want. Middle Americans that have not been influenced by regressing oppressive mentalities will rise to save this country. When America left Afghanistan, the Afghan government fell so fast because they were weak socialist appointees. The Taliban came in as the alphas and took over quickly, and now a rapidly growing alpha, ISIS, is going to take over the Taliban. That is how real takeovers work. If you think a country with many alphas is going to just roll over during a regime change, you have another thing coming. They will rise and take back what we believe is right.

America needs to be adequately prepared for the near future. If this country is going to hang their hat on depending on President Biden to keep us safe and in control of the way the world functions, we have a lot of issues ahead. Biden abandoned our people and allies in Afghanistan, turned his back on our law enforcement, softened our military with woke policies, allowed a racism flame to emblazon, and allowed our border to become a transaction for cartels. This is not going to work for our way of life if we want to keep our country prosperous.

As I've stated numerous times in this book, woke does not work. The method is very divisive and oppresses one side of the issue while empowering the other. In the international world, woke is a weakness. As our enemies become more and more militarily powerful and hardened, we become less likely able to withstand a hard-fought conflict. War is not a playground where you get punched in the face and get up and over a few days forget about what happened. It is brutal and life changing, and while our enemies prepare their soldiers for these types of battles, physically and mentally, we are too busy worrying about making sure the gay soldier feel comfortable. This is unacceptable among our ranks. You are not a black soldier or a white soldier or a gay soldier, you are an American soldier. The training angle should be the same for everyone; we should be well prepared for countries like China and Russia. American socialism is a weakness that our enemies will surely exploit quickly.

Our leaders need to see this forward, while preparing for all possible scenarios. We need to be able to trust that our military officers and commander-in-chief can lead any situation that may occur. Without intense intelligence agencies, there are no excuses plausible to explain any such situation that can surprise us. Biden needs to get out of the way and let the alphas do what they do best. I would like to think that Defense Secretary Austin and General Milley are fully capable of conducting our military accordingly, as they were both around for several presidencies. As of right now, our leadership is absent, and it has become apparent that common citizens are going to be seeking to take the lead.

In February of 2022, an armada of truck drivers banded together to drive across Canada to their capital city of Ottawa in order to protest mandatory COVID vaccines. At no time in the media coverage did there appear to be any type of uprising or violence; however, Canadian Prime Minister Justin Trudeau ordered an emergency act, which is a form of martial law, to clear out the truck drivers that flooded the streets of Ottawa. Mainstream media has painted the cowardly act as a leader taking control of a bunch of racist truck drivers, since they are all a bunch of hillbillies that kill people of color, sarcastically.

According to Wikipedia, the "Emergencies Act is a statute passed by the Parliament of Canada in 1988 which authorizes the federal government to take extraordinary 'temporary' measures to respond to public welfare emergencies, public order emergencies, international emergencies and war emergencies. The law replaces the War Measures Act passed in 1914." In its current form, the Emergencies Act has only been used once, for Canadian convoy protests. The War Measures Act has been utilized three times in its existence: WWI, WWII, and the 1970 October Crisis, where Deputy Premier Pierre Laporte and British diplomat James Cross were abducted by a liberation group. It is difficult to see how a peaceful protest of truck drivers not wanting a vaccine would generate the usage of the Emergencies Act. Apparently, PM Trudeau has a fear of big rigs.

In all seriousness, what Trudeau did was an absolute violation of everything that America believes in. In Canada, the rules are bit different; however, as the purifiers of communism and crimes against humanity, the US should not be encouraging Canada to arrest peaceful citizens, as President Joe Biden suggested in his call with Trudeau on February 11th, 2022. To me, this is one tyrant speaking to another tyrant on how to oppress and silence the grassroots of the country. PM Trudeau needs to keep in mind that those truck drivers are symbolic to his nation as they represent the great Canadians that get dirty, bloody, and make family sacrifices to keep the country functioning. They not only represent truck drivers but also farmers, factory workers, stay-at-home moms and dads, and anyone else that is just trying to get their way of life back to normal. Also note that 90 percent of the Canadian population has been vaccinated.

To the Royal Canadian Mounted Police (RCMP), you are serving a duty to your people, not the government. If you stand with communist dictator Trudeau, you in turn are tyrants that should be imprisoned right beside him. Your excuse of just following orders is no longer valid in this world, and that goes towards every single law enforcement officer in the world. We see you, and we are not impressed with that excuse anymore. Your moral compass and duty to your people supersedes your call to government. So, when your leader is a tyrant, he should be apprehended.

President Biden is also in the wrong in this situation, as he encouraged a swift and direct end to a situation at the Canadian capital that could have been avoided if PM Trudeau would have held some sort of communication with the truckers. Instead, he becomes responsible for the increased tension that occurred, still without violence, with nearly two hundred protesters being unlawfully arrested by a northern government full of cowards because PM Trudeau wants to appear relevant on the world stage. President Biden, yet again, exerted his expert ability to give faulty advice to people that can't think on their own.

This is what you see all over the world right now and into the future. You're seeing more and more revolt by the people against the government. In Glenn Beck's *The Overton Window*, he describes the system that the government uses to manipulate us to find more and more atrocities caused by the government to be socially acceptable. The Overton window is used in nearly every country to sway the people to think a certain as to move forward with an agenda. What I don't think Beck concluded was his assortation of this method just assumes that "the people" will just be a robot society and keep falling for the tricks their leaders pose. In fact, common citizens are a resilient when it comes to correcting society wrongs. There is a breaking point where the people will stop tyrannical behavior by their government.

In this country, Americans will follow their government to their deaths, as we see more and more protests on the streets by great patriots that have spent most of their lives monitoring decline of the greatest nation on the planet. These are the Americans that are at our root with their red, white, and blue blood, which will never kneel for any nation or tyrants bought out by our enemy nations. The people see what is happening. They see the price tags on Washington bureaucrats, and the signs are present that there will be a shifting or changing of the guard. The people will take their power back and realign this nation, which will create balance again.

Beck's *Overton Window* can also become a tool of common people, which is what I think is happening. We are having more and more protests, while some do get a bit hostile. As Americans sitting in front of our TVs every night watching the evening news and seeing these events unfold, it creates a more advanced norm than just having your voice heard and sending letters to congressmen and women. If the Overton Window moves again for the common people, it will lead to revolution which will be bad for the world.

It is my strategic opinion that as our Constitution prevents our military from patrolling our own streets in revolution, the cowardly government will deploy NATO to come restore order. I think leaders like Nancy Pelosi, Chuck Schumer, and Bernie Sanders think NATO is going to work well for them. What I see in the Ukraine-Russia conflict is a NATO that is scared of big bad Russia. They just sit around and praise the Ukrainians for their valiant fight against one of the greatest world powers on the planet. I have news for the oppressors of this nation, foreign and domestic; if you think the Ukrainian people are brave, wait until you see what America can do when you try to take our freedoms away. We will destroy any NATO force they send here fairly easily. Despite the broken society that the liberal left is trying to create to take our unity away, put troops on our streets from another country and you will see a nation of George Washington's emerge to eradicate everything in our path in order to reset our government.

America is very much in tune with what the Biden Administration's agenda is and where you're trying to take us. We are awake to your media propaganda that you learned from Hitler himself. We will not stand for your socialist society, nor will we allow you a free pass to tyranny. There is a price to be paid; you will answer for your infiltration into our government and society. We see you and you can no longer hide. You made a grave error in judgement when you thought we were divided enough to sneak your camouflaged agenda into the chambers of our nation real fast, but you highly miscalculated.

America is a nation of heroes that will lay down their lives for their beliefs and morality. At the end of the day, we bleed red, white, and blue. For treason-laden politicians like AlexandriaOcasio-Cortez, Ilhan Omar, Rashida Tlaib, Bernie Sanders, Barak Obama, Hillary Clinton, Joe Biden, and, hell, Hunter Biden, your time is coming, where you will feel the real wrath for betraying the United States of America. We, the people, will protect this nation from enemies of democracy both foreign and domestic. There is ample time for each one of you to turn your prospective views back towards democratic policies of freedom before you all face the tribunals and courts that lead to cold and damp prison cells.

The perspective is very clear among the American people that follow Donald Trump and rally with him. Trump is the first president to really stand up for the average American, which is why when he gives a speech in any area of the US, there are tens of thousands of people consistently there to show support. Left-wing liberals despise Trump for his charisma and arrogance because Trump is an alpha that they cannot control nor get to follow the socialist agenda. Trump's Republican Party is a sample of what political parties are supposed to look like. He is energetic, makes his own agenda, and executes his plan. Trump does have some errors in his methodology, but I do believe, overall, he is fighting for the greater good.

Maybe Trump is the savior of the country, or maybe he's a manipulative tyrant like the left wants you to believe. What is known is if Trump makes a mistake, he will be held accountable for any action that is a violation of his duty as a president, current or former. It is astounding as to how the Biden Administration has continuously dodged accountability repeatedly since day one in the White House. Just as they say in *Game of Thrones*, "the North remembers"; America remembers too.

The botched Afghanistan withdrawal will forever be remembered as the event that started the Biden downfall. Thirteen brave soldiers perished due to Biden's failures. The president has never been held accountable, nor has anyone in his administration. Sgt. Johanny Rosario Pichardo, Sgt. Nicole L. Gee, Staff Sgt. Darin T. Hoover, Cpl. Hunter Lopez, Cpl. Daegan w. Page, Cpl. Humberto A. Sanchez, Lance Cpl. David L. Espinoza, Lance Cpl. Jared M. Schmitz, Lance Cpl. Rylee J. McCollum, Lance Cpl. Dylan R. Merola, Lance Cpl. Kareem M Nikoui, Navy Corpsman Maxton W. Soviak, and Staff Sgt. Ryan C. Knauss deserve to have their answers. Those brave soldiers were left in Afghanistan with faulty leadership that cost them their lives, when it didn't have to happen at all. Joe Biden should be impeached for their deaths and charged in the military tribunal for his neglect for our soldier's lives.

After Afghanistan, we can move on to the inflation problem that Biden blames everyone but himself. Jen Psaki has coined the gas price hike as the Putin price hike, when, in fact, gas prices went up over a dollar a gallon in the first year of Biden's presidency, which occurred before Russia invaded the Ukraine. If Biden had allowed out pipelines to keep flowing, there would be better competition in the world oil market, which in turn would hav kept oil prices affordable. Biden needs to be held accountable for the inflation issues that plague every single American. I imagine when you take a more than expected portion of someone's paycheck, they will be upset with the rapid change regardless of if a democrat or republican caused it to happen. This fault is going to cost Biden his reelection bid.

We should also not forget about Biden's non-existent border policy. I have yet to see what it is that Biden has done with our border other than let everyone in. I am not against immigration; however, I am highly against an open border. Allowing everyone to just walk across into our country without a work visa or documentation is unacceptable. Our crime rates are too high as it is, and the prospect of allowing hundreds of migrants into our country with criminal records is astounding to me. There are many countries in this world, many being third-world countries, that will not allow you to enter even with a misdemeanor. With Biden removing the Title 42 provision/expulsion, immigrants will be allowed to enter the country at will, without any kind of COVID vetting. At the same time, liberals are having a fit about a federal judge ruling that mask mandates are not lawful. If there is one thing that plagues Joe Biden, it is his ability to confuse the public as to what the expectations are for COVID protocols. It appears to me that even though the CDC and Dr. Fauci state we should still be wearing masks, the law of the United States disagrees. I feel COVID is over for my age group and the age group of my children. I went mask-less the entire pandemic and didn't even get a cold, nor did anyone in my family. The study I conducted among my bloodline concluded no one in my immediate family contracted a serious case of COVID. It is a fact that most of the people in my family are in great general health, which I feel contributed to their ability to fight off the virus. With that conclusion, it is easy to understand why

I do not agree with the Biden Administration's devout passion to keep us masked up.

Americans need to keep a very close eye on several issues as election season is among us as we are months away from mid-term elections, which it is very apparent they are. Biden's Quinnipiac polls reflect the displeasure the country has for this administration. Even CNN polls are showing dissatisfaction with the president. If we look at the Quinnipiac polls since Biden took office, we can see an obvious pattern emerge.

DATE	APPROVAL
1-28-21	49%
2-11-21	50%
4-8-21	48%
5-18-21	49%
7-27-21	47%
9-10-21	44%
10-1-21	40%
10-15-21	40%
11-11-21	38%
1-7-22	35%
2-10-22	37%
2-25-22	38%
3-4-22	40%
3-24-22	38%
3-31-22	40%
4-7-22	35%
4-21-22	40%

The pattern presented shows that Biden has not recovered in polling since the Afghanistan debacle. Since then, he has floated around the high 30s to low 40 percent. At some point, I think the White

House should address the Afghanistan retreat and hold someone accountable. This would help the confidence of the American people. As of right now, Americans just do not trust Biden or anyone else in his administration. The president is untrustworthy, his son is untrustworthy, his cabinet refuses to answer questions or don't know the answers, and the VP is always laughing at the misery of everyone else. Maybe I'm an old school manager, but if I see someone is not doing well on my spreadsheet, I'm going to hold them accountable, and we are going to problem solve how to improve their department. The last thing I will do is do nothing.

Coming together to battle the failed socialist takeover by Biden and his cronies needs to come to the forefront. If moderate Democrats make their voices heard beside Republicans, it is not an act of betrayal of your party. The Democrat Party is no longer a party of democracy. It has morphed into something evil. It is my hope that this chapter has provided enough information to help you stand out among the great patriots to rid our nation of socialists. It is time to cleanse the Democrat Party.

CHAPTER 9

GOOD GUYS AND BAD GUYS

With the United States clearly divided, it is my expressed opinion that, as readers, you should all know with certainty who the real heroes and villains are in this real-time story. As we look at the differences in media and several individuals that I will dissect, decide whether Republican or Democrat as to what is right or wrong in your own moral compass.

The media is a two-way street, with most of the outlets being very liberal, while the rest have a conservative tint to them. CNN is the leader of the extreme liberal media. I remember growing up, CNN was a fair news network that would lean moderate and examine all side of issues. Today, the network has a lot of issues that I'm not sure they will recover from. When I sit and watch CNN for a period, I hear a lot of the same no matter what anchor or segment is on. They tend to focus on oppressive issues that revolve around silencing large groups of Americans. They have a distinct fear that the left does not have enough competitive candidates to compete in elections upcoming and near future.

CNN is the largest culprit; however, MSNBC, NBC, ABC, *Washington Post*, and *New York Times* have also made my list of extreme left networks and publications. I don't see them talking to very many current democrat politicians because, I believe, they don't want to expose the true agenda. Their focus is on poking conservative politicians like President Trump, Florida governor Ron DeSantis, Senator Ted Cruz, etc. Historically, conservative leaders will look away and let the democrats run their agendas. Today, conservatives have banded together and have fought back, as I think they now understand the severity of the liberal socialist movement which is a threat to our historical democracy. The media plays into that ideology and panders falsehoods that will never be factchecked, due to the liberal media owns the factcheckers.

As all the liberal media outlets are at fault, CNN gets most of the conservative scrutiny due to their repeated scandals of 2021 with Chris Cuomo's issues, sexual accusations against several executives, and the resignation of CNN president Jeff Zucker. The network is full of anchors and employees that love to throw stones at conservatives, while living in a glass house. It appears that glass is starting to crack, as their ratings are down and the public just plainly doesn't trust their one-sided reporting.

The other angle of the media influence towards Americans comes from conservative-minded networks and publications. Fox News spent the majority of 2021 as the top-rated news network on cable TV. Obviously, this means that more Americans are receiving their news from a conservative angle, rather than the left- or moderate-leaning media outlets. As Fox News has positioned themselves as the network for historical American values, they have not always been a solid network. During the Trump presidency, the network appeared to be divided among anchors and choice of guests. Anchors like Tucker Carlson and Sean Hannity heavily supported President Trump, while some of the others were a little skeptical of the former president's methods and overconfident ways of speaking to Americans, especially the media.

It does appear as we have shifted the country into a liberal sense of governing, Fox News has united in their support for President Trump. As the Biden Administration enters their second year in office, conservative media banded together as a greater enemy has emerged among our own soil.

Bernie Sanders made a lot of headway for the United States socialist movement during the 2016 presidential election season. Eventually, he was weeded out by Hillary Clinton, but his influence jumpstarted a movement that had been in the works for decades. As a self-identified "democratic socialist," he believes we need to "create an economy that works for all, not just the very wealthy." This sounds fine and dandy, but capitalism is already set up to all for all Americans to financially succeed. It would be appropriate to see what he is really saying and not just a very watered-down version of how Americans should only live off of the handouts the government issues every month while our government coffers are enlarged by the theft of funds from the free citizens of the US.

Sanders is also supported by many high-ranking members of Black Lives Matter. This is significant and not at all surprising since BLM is founded on the Marxist agenda, which is a close methodology to Bernie Sanders' socialist belief system. This movement is attracted to Bernie Sanders for several reasons: the promotion of a lot of free handouts from the government, an adjustment to the wealthy, cleaner environment, delegation of trillions of dollars to millennial-friendly causes.

The problem that Sanders is not accounting for with such groups as BLM is that his methods are not going to solve the root problem of African American issues, which consists of greater education in at-risk communities, ending gang violence, family unity. These issues have been a plague to good people for decades, and every president has promised to address them, which resulted in no effort at all to make a difference. Sanders is no different; he's a tyrant of democracy with an ideal that alpha countries like China and Russia will exploit in a second. His form of socialism weakens the American soul by taking the dream of prosperity away from the heart of America. Weak people led by a weak government will be catastrophic.

Alexandria Ocasio Cortez is a minuscule mind that is a tool for Bernie Sanders to maneuver around and make noise like a bull horn. Her ideals are just an echo of what has already failed, which progressives keep trying to push. Her following consists of mostly collegiate hipsters that fear difficult world situations. As the leader of "The Squad," which consists of Cortez, Rashida Tlaib, Ilhan Omar, Ayanna Pressley, Jamaal Bowman, and Cori Bush, AOC elevates issues brought forward as if they are being talked about by a bunch of whiney college kids that have never experienced real life. Everyone can agree that the climate is an issue and we all can do better to clean up our air, but, contradictory, China produces more CO_2 emissions than any other nation, and "The Squad" makes no case as to sanctioning suggestions with the great Red Panda. In fact, they avoid talking negatively about China at all costs, due to the reality that they have no international clout to take on such a superpower as China. AOC's power is only enriched by a left-wing media agenda that the rest of the world laughs at.

When you add AOC and Bernie Sanders together, they are going to be named singlehandedly responsible for the destruction of the Democrat Party. Their view does not resonate among the populous, which only leads them to a minority that does not understand America and world politics. It is no surprise since democrats have been leaning in this direction for a long time. It comes down to typical weak-minded academia trying to outsmart alphas into the bidding, which we have presently learned does not work. Bill Clinton even dodged the draft and fled to Canada instead of fighting for our country against the communist Vietnam. In today's standards, President Clinton lacks a lot of the fortitude that Ukrainian President Zelenskyy and the Ukrainians put on display for the world.

Nancy Pelosi also makes my list of tyrants and cowards among the American political system. Although she is the face of the House of Representatives, she has not one single original idea left in her head. She is merely a mouth for those socialist behind the scenes. She does reveal the hierarchy behind the scenes. When President Biden doesn't push the issues that "The Squad" deems important, Nancy will quickly align herself with the president, which tells me that Biden does in fact have a powerful voice in Democrat Party. I do still feel that Biden only speaks when Obama says speak. Nancy Pelosi is only in Congress for her own personal gain, as her husband has been getting inside investment tips through his House Majority Leader wife for years. As far as being evil, I don't think Pelosi fits that category, but she will look out for number one, whether that is her or the Democrat president that is in office.

Barak Obama is a focal point with a lot of issues in the world today as President Biden has been making it his legacy to bring back every failed idea Obama implemented and coined as his own. While in office, he utilized minority vote to gain power until they had no use for him and ignored the very voters that lifted him to the presidency. Obama's clear plan was to make America a socialist nation by implementing phasing out of various rights that he thought he could disguise as helping America. One of the biggest impacts during his presidency was to implement Obamacare. This appeared to be a great idea on paper, and Obama spoke to the media about how great his idea was. Obamacare was clearly implemented to emulate the European medical insurance, where the government had more control over medical costs. This appears to be a grand idea; however, the insurance ended up not being as affordable as the administration would like you to think and it was very confusing to navigate. The fact is that if we do not allow for free-market pricing, doctors will not make as much money and will likely move to other nations that have no market cap on insurance. This will lead America with a healthcare system that is not elite.

The biggest dark cloud of President Obama is not so much the little things he did that seemed to lean socialist but where his mindset came from. When Obama was up for re-election in 2012, one of his endorsements came from the Communist Party USA. This is significant because an organization is not going to just endorse anyone. They are going to place their stamp on the candidate they believe will represent their views. President Obama's communist ties go all the way back to his childhood in Hawaii, growing up with known Communist Party USA member Frank Marshall Davis. According to key-wiki.org, in March of 2001 a speech by another Communist Party USA supporter, Gerald Horne, named Obama as a tie to the Communist Party USA, as well as Frank Marshall Davis.

It shows how deep Obama's influence was in the US government pre-presidency, as it is a violation of the creed every member of our armed forces promises to protect, to be a known affiliate of communism all while holding office. Barak Obama is a communist and should have never been allowed to run for president. Our country has become so lax in our assessments of our politicians that we are allowing those that are anti-democracy to become president. Yes, Obama has stated he is not a communist; however, is this not how communist Russia tried to infiltrate our country during the Cold War? If our government officials at the time had done what they should have done, Obama would have been exposed and barred from running for office. Instead, he is the clear puppet master of Joe Biden.

Joy Reid is a very menial nobody, but she tries to set so many obvious fires in our country that I had to speak my peace on this woman. Joy Reid is an MSNBC TV anchor, 1991 Harvard graduate, author, and certified tool for Marxist tyrants. I find it very funny to read the titles of two of her books; *Fracture: Barak Obama, the Clintons, and the Racial Divide*; *The Man Who Sold America: Trump and the Unraveling of the American Story*. At least with *Fracture*, she understood that Obama and the Clintons caused a racial divide. Both Clinton and Obama campaigned on the empty promises that they would lift the African American community from the impoverished cesspool that most of them find themselves in. In fact, every single American president has abandoned this very sentiment except Donald Trump. Joy Reid, can you please acknowledge the amount of good Trump did for the African American communities? Look at all the money he dumped into all-black educational institutions for higher learning. Look at the minority unemployment rate during his mere four years as president. Donald Trump put a lot of money in the lower class of the African American community by investing in their education and skilled jobs.

I really like her title *The Man Who Sold America: Trump and the Unraveling of the American Story*. Mind you, I'm not going to spend the $4.25 needed to purchase these sad excuses for books to understand what kind of left-sided propaganda that is installed in them; however, I will speak on the titles. At what point did Donald Trump sell America? For the four years he was in office, Democrats pursued the big lie they peddled about Russian Collusion, and I do hope people go to prison for their roles in that lie to the American people. Joy Reid, you're an admitted democrat who also spoke on the Trump-Russia collusion, falsely. It would be very honorable of you to admit your wrongdoings and apologize to the former president of the United States. I know your proud Harvard degree prevents you from every admitting you are wrong, and that's okay. Maybe you'll get to go to prison also. President Trump took us out of the spending too much money on NATO while European "allies" paid very little. Look how well that turned out as they sit on the border as innocent Ukrainians beg for help, just to be turned away as Putin massacres their people.

But as you stated, Ms. Reid, whom you call yourself on Twitter as pro-democracy as you support Marxist BLM, "We don't need to ask ourselves if the international response would be the same if Russia unleashed their horror on a country that wasn't white and largely Christian, because Russia has already done it." If you don't understand the difference of a conflict in the Ukraine with Russia versus a conflict in Yemen, you are completely out of touch with society. In case you need to be told, Russia has a lot of nuclear weapons with a leader that, I believe, is not afraid to use them. I do understand the point, an atrocity is an atrocity no matter what color everyone is; however, the focal point is on Russia right now. They could reach out and touch anyone they want with a nuke. No one in the Middle East is enough of a nuclear threat that we cannot handle in the US. That's the difference: Russia, over six thousand nukes, Saudi Arabia, zero!

Ms. Reid, if you are unhappy with the current situation in Russia, maybe you should press your great coward, I mean leader, Joe Biden to change course and let Europe deal with the Russia-Ukraine conflict while we shift gears towards Yemen. I would be absolutely in favor of that; however, as everyone in America knows, Biden has conflict with the Ukraine, Russia, and Saudi Arabia. He did ask the Saudis for increased oil production in early March.

It is obvious that Joy Reid is a direct BLM Marxist spokesman. She spends most of her airtime whining and complaining about inequalities of the African American communities. It is rightly so to stand up for minority groups, however don't weaponize them. Go in and make a difference in someone's life in an at-risk community. Hopefully that kind of work is not too far below your false celebrity status and Harvard degree.

Kamala Harris is most likely the least qualified vice president I have ever seen. Mainstream media is responsible for her uprising into power. Her record as a senator and attorney general in California falls in line with the majority of the typical West Coast politicians: ban weapons, progressive tax policies, healthcare reform, etc. What really sticks out to me, when it comes to her positions in the legal system, is her time as the chief of the Career Criminal Division, where she supervised five other attorneys to look into mainly major criminal offences and three strikes offenders. This is a very strict law when it comes to repeat offenders in California, and Kamala Harris was responsible for enforcing this law.

Personally, I am not opposed to the three strikes law, as it greatly deters an increase of recidivism, so for Harris to completely avoid condoning criminals during riots is unspeakable and encourages anarchy. Further, when Harris ran for District Attorney in 2002 against

Terrence Hallinan, the incumbent, she argued that his 52 percent conviction rate was not sufficient to be district attorney in the future when the state rate was around 83 percent. Harris went on to win the election by a large margin with her push for more convictions. As she became settled into her DA chair, she also "pushed for higher bail for criminal defendants involved in gun-related crimes, arguing that historically low bail encouraged outsiders to commit crimes in San Francisco." It is interesting that as much legal expertise that she has, President Biden would not utilize her in a more neutral role when dealing with the growing number of crimes in the US.

Harris did have several programs that I support and don't understand why she is not putting her created platforms on display for the nation to somewhat follow. Her program for re-entry was very successful, considering the high rates of recidivism that occurs once an offender commits their first crime. The "Back on Track" program was intense and had a target age group of eighteen to thirty years old. This is a smart way to really attack a problem, as this is the age group that is most likely to reoffend. If the offender was a nonviolent offender, at the completion of her program, she would recommend that the offender's felony conviction would be expunged. The program was cost efficient to taxpayers and had a lot of success.

In 2006, she implemented a truancy initiative to help combat violent crimes that involved youth in at-risk communities. This is one of few programs that politicians try to peddle to gain votes but expect little return; however, Harris put a lot of time and effort into attacking problems in the troubled communities that have high violent crime rates. I can applaud her efforts in this aspect as I think when we talk about root-cause issues, she enacted a strong program to deter crime at its root.

From 2011 to 2013 VP Harris attacked the lending practices of mortgage brokers that were aggressively foreclosing on constituents and had a lot of success in litigation as huge settlements were rewarded to mortgage holders that were foreclosed on. This is a big task to go up against large financial institutions such as SunTrust, Bank of America, and JP Morgan. The only mistake that I see that she made was by taking money from OneWest Bank head Steve Mnuchin, who went on to become US treasury secretary. Mnuchin at the time was being accused of "widespread violation" of California foreclosure laws.

As attorney general of California, Harris attacked border issues when it came to cartels and human trafficking. She passed several pieces of legislation that would allow for communications between California and the northwest regions of Mexico. She clearly understood the evils of transnational gang activity and the chaos it creates in border states. This was a very aggressive stance that now California politicians disagree with, which makes me think that either VP Harris doesn't really agree with Biden's stance on immigration policies or she's good at saying and doing what her constituents want.

Her stance on immigration drastically changed when she became elected to the US Senate in 2017, becoming an anti-Trump policy maker, even though a lot of what she did as Attorney General of California matched up with Trump's immigration views. I must ask, what changed? The answer is clear that as she became a rising star in California, Nancy Pelosi started to attach herself to a lot of the endorsing of Harris. So, when Harris became a Democratic Member of the US Senate, she had to either join the club all the way or be defeated and the Pelosi-led democrats control all seats in California in democratic areas.

VP Harris's time in the US Senate from 2017–2021 was spent in the Senate Judiciary Committee investigating President Trump and wasting taxpayers' dollars. Interestingly enough, in 2019 she publicly claimed, "voter suppression prevented Democrats Stacey Abrams and Andrew Gillum from winning the 2018 gubernatorial elections in Georgia and Florida; Abrams lost by 55,000 votes." Law expert Richard L. Hasan later stated, "I have seen no good evidence that the suppressive effects of strict voting and registration laws affected the outcome of the governor's races in Georgia and Florida."

In July of that same year, Harris joined a bipartisan effort to "urge the Trump administration to investigate the allegations of Uyghur genocide by the Chinese Communist Party." If we are a country of standing up for what's right, then why is Kamala Harris the only Democrat that is standing up against China? I think what she did at that time was valiant and should be commended.

As her time as vice president is still ongoing, her support among Americans is dwindling by the day. I think there are several factors that facilitate as to why she is under the water in polls. I also have a theory as to what she could do to increase her influence. First, the consensus among most Republicans is that Harris is only in the position of vice president because she's a woman and of color. This is Biden's constant way of thinking, which to me appears that he is only seeing people by their color.

One factor that has Harris looking incompetent is her public speaking. She comes across as a cackling buffoon most of the time, even in times of crisis. She also has no realistic solutions to the trouble that most Americans face. It is also very easy to note that the senior officials in the White House do not take her seriously. As a minority woman that, according to her previous record, especially her legal career, it is very difficult to see her pride allows her to be the laughing-stock of the United States.

Biden did have to utilize her in several major issues that not many Americans realize that the VP is very qualified to tackle. Biden put her in charge of working with the Central American countries of Guatemala, Honduras, and El Salvador, knowing that stopping massively funded convoys funded by George Soros will be stopped from migrating north to our southern border. Harris's role in this was merely a stall tactic and roleplay, with no real solution sought by the Biden Administration. From Kamala's tenure as attorney general in California, she has already fought this battle rigorously, so it is very disturbing to see her half-ass this issue when the majority of Americans see this as a huge security risk.

After America realized the White House has no real intention of securing the border, Biden then sent VP Harris to Europe to make a good faith effort to show Ukraine they will support their fight against Russia, but from a distance. The issue that hurt her in Europe was a press conference with the president of Poland about immigration issues in which Harris continued to do her infamous cackle, which did not translate well to the American and European people.

To summarize the situation that Kamala Harris faces, when you look at it as isolated incidents that add up to my assessment, Harris is not on my bad-guy list. The root of her being leans more republican, so I'm not real sure how America labeled her as the most liberal politician in the Senate at the time. She is tough on crime and very active in her field of study in a conservative way, especially when it comes to immigration crime. What I think happened to her as she rose in the Democrat party: She had all the intangibles that the socialist movement needed to help Biden move the country forward in their agenda. I'd be willing to bet that she was told to just follow the script.

Kamala Harris is in a unique position. I think she should drop the Democrats' socialist agenda and quit playing to the agenda. She needs to step to the front, as Biden is not competent enough to lead this country to the forefront of the world. If she would come out and implement tough on crime stances and getting the border secure, she would instill a lot of confidence into the voters of this country. Her legacy as a politician is viewed as a giant failure when, in fact, she has all the tools and fresh ideas that are semi-conservative and semi-moderate Democrat. If she can accomplish this and turn back on the energy independence oil drilling for the American People, she would elevate herself to a new high that would likely make her president as a Republican.

President Joe Biden is the exact epiphany of a washed-up, corrupt politician that is very much past his prime. It doesn't make much sense that the left would hang all their decades of planning on an outdated, incoherent tyrant. This man should have retired from politics decades ago as his core principles are far from on point to today's standards.

Every decade Biden was in the Senate, he targeted a different culture group it seems. In 1993, "Biden voted for a provision that deemed homosexuality incompatible with military life, thereby banning gays from serving in the armed forces." In 1996, "he voted for the Defense of Marriage Act, which prohibited the federal government from recognizing same-sex marriages, thereby barring individuals in such marriages from equal protection under federal law and allowing states to do the same." Luckily, in 2015 the US Supreme Court ruled that the Defense of Marriage Act was unconstitutional.

The '70s provided a great opportunity for Biden to wage a war on African Americans rights. In 1974, "Biden voted to table a proposal containing anti-busing and anti-desegregation clauses but later voted for a modified version containing a qualification that it was not intended to weaken the judiciary's power to enforce the 5th Amendment and the 14th Amendment." The very next year in 1975, "he supported a proposal that would have prevented the Department of Health, Education, and Welfare from cutting federal funds to districts that refused to integrate, he said busing was a bankrupt idea [violating] the cardinal rule of common sense and that his opposition would make it easier for other liberals to follow suit." In other words, Biden spent a lot of his Senate time in the '70s oppressing the African American communities.

During the Gulf War of 1991, Biden was opposed to the invasion, due to the US taking most of the financial responsibility, but later supported a massive bombing of Bosnia with the help of NATO, which the US heavily funds. He appears to be very wishy washy in his approach to international politics. I believe, now openly knowing his financial gains from other nations, that he was in a position to pick and choose his stance on the world stage based on who was paying.

Biden also had several international successes, while helping the Clinton Administration coordinate a peace agreement between Ireland and the UK in 1998. In 1999 he then targeted Kosovo and Slobodan Milosevic. After 9/11, Biden became highly supportive of an invasion in Afghanistan and then later agreed for the US to "elimi-nate" Saddam Hussein. Later on he criticized President George HW Bush on not being upfront on the cost and timeframe of the invasions.

To call Biden's Senate career a complete failure is not quite accu-rate. It would be better defined as a complete disaster. It is very sus-pect that the Democrats repeatedly put Biden in the presidential pool as much of a flawed candidate he is on paper. However, when your party controls the stream of information that the public relies on, it becomes a huge strategic advantage. To me, it is no surprise that Biden's first year was a tornado of failures on everything he touched.

It is a fine line between good guys and bad guys in American pol-itics. Donald Trump most likely fits both of those molds more accu-rately than any of the previous individuals talked about in this chapter. It seemed that before the 2016 election, Trump could do no wrong and everything he touched appeared to achieve a lot of success. He had the top reality show on TV, his business was doing exceptionally well, and he was well liked by the majority of the US. Things changed for him dramatically when he won the Republican primary, which then led to his presidency. Trump immediately became attacked heavily by the Clinton corruption mafia and the Nazi propagandists' mainstream media.

The attack on Trump began when the Clinton Campaign con-cocted the false narrative that Trump colluded with Russian President Vladimir Putin to rig the election. After the release of the Durham Report, America now knows this to be untrue. Several people in the Clinton circle were indicted initially, with the expectation that more indictments are to come.

December 18, 2019, the House of Representatives voted to im-peach President Trump for abuse of power and obstruction. Many Americans don't realize how Congress works, which is what I think the Democrats expected as the Senate later voted to acquit the pres-ident. The damage had been done, and voters that are ignorant to what really happened in Trump's first impeachment don't realize that

Trump, in fact, was not legally impeached. The plot by the Democrats worked and created a mantra around Trump that he was a corrupt bully that was in bed with several nations, including Ukraine, which is what the impeachment was about.

The accusations claim that Trump used his international influence to withhold aid and access to the Ukraine and President Zelensky. Zelensky, however, agreed with President Trump that this is not how the conversation took place. To summarize a long story, Trump was acquitted in the Senate, and he then fired the whistleblowers from their respective positions within the US Government. My take on this event, as the media continued to cry corruption, if my closest advisors started to tell on me, I'd get rid of them too. As a president, you should have people that you can always trust around you, not tyrants that betray their leader. It is obvious Alexander Vindman and Gordon Sondland have no idea how a strong nation is built. On top of the acquittal, with Zelensky being newly elected as president of Ukraine, succeeding a long line of extremely corrupt presidents, Trump was in the correct position to deny instant aid to a country with a history of misconduct and corruption.

Trump's second impeachment that happened after the January 6th insurrection in 2021 will forever tarnish Trump as, if he seeks the presidency again in 2024, Democrats will most definitely make the incident a large talking point. With their control over most of the media outlets in the world, changing the minds of one-sided Americans will be a large task. The media simply portrays January 6th to be summarized as such: Trump spoke and then advised the mass to march to the Capitol Building and "fight like hell." Then the insurrection happened, and people were assaulted and killed.

For those of you that have not seen the timeline of how this really happened, I will attempt to explain to you who, what, when, and how. At 10:58 A.M., several militias, including the Proud Boys, arrived at the Capitol to take position. Twelve noon, Donald Trump spoke to thousands of people at the Ellipse, which is very close to the White

House. The walk from this location would take thirty-five minutes at best. At 12:53 P.M., the crowds at the Capitol became enlarged as Trump was still giving his speech several blocks away. 1:10 P.M., Trump's speech ends, and within minutes Americans breached the Capitol grounds as Capitol security called for back-up. As the timeline shows, there is no way Trump's group of supporters that he spoke to could have made it to the Capitol that day in time for the initial altercation at the barrier around the Capitol. The actual breach of the Capitol grounds occurred at 1:45 P.M., which Trump's mass could have been there for. At 2:13 P.M., Americans breached the Capitol Building uncontested and roamed the Capitol Chamber.

There are several notable deaths in this situation, Brian Sicknick, Capitol Police Officer, died from the assault that occurred that day. Ashli Babbitt was the woman in the infamous video of the Secret Service agent cowardly firing on the unarmed Babbitt. As a former Air Force veteran, she had every right from her duty to this country to have her voice heard and not murdered while unarmed by a Secret Service agent that is likely awarded expert marksmanship and therefore fully capable of maiming Babbitt without death.

Taking away the conspiracies that surround Trump and the Capitol Riot, which included planted federal agents to help incite the riot, which I do believe occurred. President Trump built up the January 6th rally weeks before it happened. It clearly was not a big secret that Trump was bringing tens of thousands of people together in one place. Overall, when Trump held rallies, there were no acts of violence against anyone. So, for that to change tells me something else changed. In hindsight, Trump advertised this event like he was promoting a large concert venue. Everyone in the country knew it was going to happen.

With the largest intelligence community in the world, which claims to be the best, it is extremely hard to believe the FBI, CIA, DHS, DOJ, and any other three letter acronyms could miss the opportunity to get ahead of the potential chaos that could occur. Our military puts countless hours into planning and calculating civilian casualties before striking. Overall, they are very efficient at what they do, so to say our government agencies could not get ahead of the estimated eighty thousand people in support of the forty-fifth president. Ahead of time, Trump organizers published an expected thirty thousand people to attend the rally. All the information was there for intelligence agencies to stay ahead of the insurrection. The fact that Trump was viewed by Democrats as a national security threat suggests they see him as very dangerous, so when Trump advertises a rally to overturn the election, there should have been several thousand federal law enforcement agents on the ground to maintain security of one of the most important buildings with the most important people on earth in it. Capitol Police requested it ahead of time, and Pelosi did nothing.

It is very clear to me that Trump strongly advocated for peaceful protest weeks and hours before the violence occurred. An immense amount or responsibility should fall on the government officials that knew about the event and did not proactively plan accordingly. Nancy Pelosi should be charged with neglect of duty as it was her call to make. Every head of every government intelligence agency should be removed and charged with neglect also.

Can we look at Trump as the bad guy in his two impeachment hearings? The first round has since been proven to be false, which we can now say that Trump was in the right. The "Capitol Insurrection" is still up for debate and depends on what side of the story you are on. Yes, there were calls for Trump to speak to the people at the Capitol Building to calm the protesters and he did not do that, which I believe to be neglectful for a sitting president. As for if he is responsible for the protest, no, I think there are several other individuals that deserve the blame for that infamous day rather than President Trump.

When we look at Trump's policies and campaign promises, I think it is safe to say they were highly successful. Trump rebounded our economy from the recession he inherited from the Obama Administration. In fact, his corporate tax breaks brought companies back from overseas to create better paying jobs for Americans rather than lower-paying, almost slave labor jobs for foreign companies. Personally, I made more money during the Trump presidency than under any other president during my lifespan. Economically, America took a leap ahead of all our global competitors, including China.

Trump's international stance when it comes to NATO received a huge approval from not only me but among most voters. It is absurd that US taxpayers are funding an organization that does not directly benefit our country. According to the BBC, when Trump took office the US was paying nearly 22 percent of the defense budget for NATO, which out-totaled all other NATO nations. After the organization renegotiated the disbursements, the US now contributes a little over 16 percent, which matches Germany. Before the deal was made, this was not a good situation for the US economically. The US should not fit most of the bill to fund an international defense military when we are not spending enough to build up our own military. Today, it appears that the US is spending their fair share, especially considering I feel NATO is full of spineless cowards that only want to defend countries that have third-world opposition.

The border policy will forever be an issue as it has been for decades and through numerous administrations. I do think Trump did it exactly right, as he stopped the major flow of migrants entering the country illegally and allowed for a more enforceable system to allowing migrants to enter the country the right way, which allows for authorities to properly vet people seeking visas. What Biden did in the first week of his presidency at the border is going to go down as one of the most unamerican acts in our history, right next to leaving Americans and allies to die in Afghanistan. You would think that after terrorists flew two planes into our Twin Towers we would have a better view on how important a secure border is. Instead, our president has allowed anyone to come through unvetted and thrown on the streets. Don't forget all the kids in cages.

If we are to judge a president on his ego and how he speaks to people that confront him with all the lies they have thrown at him, then I guess you can say Trump didn't do so well in that aspect; however, if we really take a look at the policies he created, it is easy to see we had a president that really took America to the next level of international success by strengthening our financial base. Trump overall is an exceptional president that lost the battle with socialism and Nazi propaganda media in the end.

When Tesla became released for distribution, that was the first time I had ever heard of Elon Musk. From a small start-up business, Zip2, to one of the frontrunners in the electric auto industry with his Tesla line, Musk has rapidly elevated his stock in the world all the way to the top as the wealthiest human on earth. I think when you really look at what Musk is doing as far as his maneuvering within the worldview, the South African has an obvious pattern that I feel is going to emerge in a big way.

When Musk created Zip2 with his brother Kimbal and Greg Kouri, there didn't seem to be an agenda in his early career other than to create a digital service that the world would be interested in, while making money. Little did he know, Compaq would buy out his company for $307 million. Musk then co-founded X.com, which was a smaller form of PayPal, which Musk eventually would merge with PayPal. After several run-ins with PayPal CEO Peter Thiel, Musk and PayPal eventually was bought out by eBay, which paid out Musk a cool $175.8 million. Three years later in 2002, Musk created Space Exploration Technologies Corp., which we all know as SpaceX.

Elon Musk has built himself a giant empire that no modern billionaire can compete with. His mind is just too far advanced, while his popularity among general Americans is almost Trump-like as he can make or break a company with a simple tweet. With his recent purchase of Twitter, Democrats are in a panic because their free reign to censor anyone that opposes their agenda is gone. Musk even stated that he is not buying Twitter to make money but instead to end censorship.

Musk is still a very unknown to me. I don't believe there is anyone on this planet that knows what his true end agenda is going to be; however, when the master plan does emerge, it will be well beyond our understanding. As time goes by, I will continue to monitor what Musk does and what I think that means for Americans. I am very hesitant to fully back him, due to the history of most political figures that look like they are doing something for the people but in turn are just leading them into their own manipulations. I think Trump had the same issues when he first started gaining ground in the 2016 presidential race. I do hold out hope that Elon Musk is a difference maker and trendsetter that he has already proven he is. I think politicians in general are deathly scared of him because his wealth allows him to set the stage as to what he sees fit. When we allow people to have that much money and influence, we are really threading the needle in hopes they have a pure heart towards us commoners. As of right now, it is impressive how Musk is creating a balance that both parties have needed. The complete jury is still out on Musk as we see how his future unfolds against a well-oiled political machine that he is surely to face soon.

Covering some of the big players in America in 2022 and deciding who is who in the real world and not what we are fed to believe by mainstream media, it is important to develop our own investigation methods and dig up the extra history on these players so we are prepared to back worthy individuals without negative surprises that may surface. I could continue to add more and more good guys and bad guys to this chapter; however, I wanted to really highlight the top American players so we have some information to ponder as election season is upon us.

CHAPTER 10

MAKING OF A DICTATOR

When we look at dictators and socialist leaders of the past, we can see several obvious characteristics that each leader possesses. In this chapter, we will look at the physical, mental, and genetic characteristics that make these individuals stand out among other great leaders in the history of the world while comparing to what will allow success today.

After looking at several significant leaders from the past and present, I found a common similarity among their physical stature in relation to their role in overall society. These leaders can easily be separated from good and evil merely based on their height. In the following excerpt, you will clearly see the comparison, keep in mind, I am 5'6".

Kaiser Wilhelm (Former Emperor of Germany)	5'3"
Manuel Noriega (Former Military Leader of Panama)	5'6"
Napoleon Bonaparte (Former Military Leader of France)	5'6"
Volodymyr Zelensky (Current President of Ukraine)	5'7"
Vladimir Putin (Current President of Russia)	5'7"
Adolf Hitler (Former Fuhrer of Germany)	5'7"
Benito Mussolini (Former PM of Italy)	5'7"
Julius Caesar (Former Dictator of Roman Empire)	5'7"
Kim Jong-un (Current Supreme Leader of N. Korea)	5'7"

Hunter Biden (Son of President Joe Biden)	5'8"
Hugo Chavez (Former President of Venezuela)	5'8"
Theodore Roosevelt (Former US President)	5'10"
Xi Jinping (Current President of China)	5'11"
Joe Biden (Current President of the US)	6'0"
George W Bush (Former President of the US)	6'0"
John F. Kennedy (Former President of the US)	6'1"
Ronald Reagan (Former President of the US)	6'1"
Barak Obama (Former President of the US)	6'2"
Bill Clinton (Former President of the US)	6'2"
George Washington (Former President of the US)	6'2"
Donald Trump (Former President of the US)	6'3"
Fidel Castro (Former President of Cuba)	6'3"
Abraham Lincoln (Former President of the US)	6'4"
Xerxes (Former King of the Persian Empire)	8'5"

Merriam-Webster.com describes Napoleon Complex as: "a domineering or aggressive attitude perceived as a form of overcompensation for being physically small or short." It is safe to say that this small bit of research is found to be accurate. Most of the American Presidents noted are six feet or taller, except for Teddy Roosevelt. Every single political or military dictator on my list is under six feet tall except Fidel Castro. In fact, it can be seen where nearly all of them fall in the five-seven to five-eight category.

From personal experience, being one of the smallest athletes on every sports team I ever played on, I had to resort to being bigger mentally and aggressively. This allowed me to excel in areas where my size would have otherwise restricted me from being relevant to my teams. In leading masses of people as these leaders have done, it is likely that they utilized the Napoleon Complex to further their agendas, whether intentionally or by genetic design.

It is very notable that Hunter Biden, with all his evil peril, fits the physical stature of the worst of dictators. Talking about Hunter Biden has not been a priority because I didn't really want to give him credit for anything, whether good or bad. As we learn more about all of the dirty deeds he is involved in around the world with some of the greatest American enemies, it is apparent that Biden is a junkie scumbag that rides the coattail of his famous father. I believe he belongs in a prison cell. If the Department of Justice would do their job, Merrick Garland, Hunter would be in prison right beside his uncle and father. It truly disturbs me how anyone in the country can be accountable for their actions except the 1 percent. It's even more sickening that if a very loud whistleblower had not come forward, Jeffery Epstein would still be running around with the most powerful people in the world selling minors. It was no secret for over a decade what his agenda was, which is what is very problematic as to who associated with him still.

Moving forward, what makes a dictator with Napoleon Complex evil? I found an interesting article published on anxiety.org, written by Seth Davin Norrholm, PhD, from Wayne State University and Samuel Hunley, PhD, from Emory University. They state, "They [dictators] see themselves as very special people, deserving of admiration and, consequently, have difficulty empathizing with he feelings and needs of others… Not only do dictators commonly show a pervasive pattern of grandiosity, they also tend to behave with a vindictiveness often observed in narcissistic personality disorder." I agree in whole with their assessment of dictators in general. It makes complete sense that most dictators are narcissists, as they generally only like themselves while trusting only their own thoughts, which can be deadly if there is any kind of resistance to their opinions.

Hunley and Norrholm further stated that "these individuals also tended to suffer from excessive anxiety- most regarding paranoid fears of citizens uprising and/or assassination." Several examples of dictatorial paranoia include the following passages.

"Saddam Hussein Displayed a level of paranoia so great the he had multiple meals prepared for him across the Iraqi land each day to ensure that no one knew where he was eating. He even went as far as to employ surgically altered body doubles."

"Kim Jong-il, the former leader of North Korea and the father of current leader Kim Jong-un, exhibited such an excessive fear of assassination while flying that he exclusively traveled via an armor-plated train, including when he traveled as far as Moscow."

"Than Shwe, a Burmese dictator, was so concerned about the tenuous nature of his rule that he once moved the capital of Burma to a remote location in the jungle without running water or electricity; an extreme tactic that was spurred on by the advice of his personal astrologer."

Another characteristic that several dictators possess is their belief that they are in some way a savior to whatever their beliefs are. Hunley and Norrholm state, "a large number of these individuals also maintained a cultural and political environment that fed grand delusions regarding their self-importance. For instance, Saddam Hussein thought of himself as the savior of the Iraqi people. Muammar Gaddafi once had himself crowned the King of Kings of Africa, and the North Korean line of succession proclaimed themselves to be almost god-like." Even though these individuals had a devout belief system that they were somehow almost divine, they still were vulnerable to their own minds as the anxiety and paranoia took hold and affected their decision-making abilities. After all, these individuals were considered some of the most dangerous people in the world in their time, which created many enemies that wished for their deaths and most certainly attempted to achieve such a feat.

When we further spiral down Hunley and Norrholm's dictatorship rabbit hole, they noted that vindictiveness will also factor in as it correlates with narcissism.

Not only do dictators commonly show a pervasive pattern of grandiosity, they also tend to behave with a vindictiveness often observed in narcissistic personality disorder. For instance, in now famous psychological experiments, researchers found that highly narcissistic individuals were more likely to try to punish those individuals who negatively evaluated their work, even when the narcissistic person believed they were administering painful electric shocks. More recent work shows that, after a negative evaluation, narcissistic people will demonstrate greater aggression even to individuals unrelated to the feedback. Such experiments can help us understand the aggressive behavior of dictators, who are known to lash out against negative evaluations.

In short, dictators with narcissistic behaviors will often lash out and punish anyone for any reason in response to the negative criticism.

Our intelligence agencies have also spent a lot of time diagnosing world leaders for all over the world with, what I feel, incredible accuracy. The CIA gave Russian President Vladimir Putin an autism diagnosis initially; however, in my experience as to how calm he appears to be in public, that does not seem to be accurate. The Office of Net Assessment's Body Leads project, according to motherjones.com, observed extensive research of Putin's behavior revealed "that the Russian President carries a neurological abnormality... identified by leading neuroscientists as Asperger's Syndrome, an autistic disorder which affects all of his decisions."

My family seems to have a male trend where Asperger's Syndrome is dominant in our daily lives. It never occurred to me that our behavior was different from other families until my youngest had obvious behavioral issues; however, intellectually, he was brilliant compared to most kids even older than he. Eventually, I took him to a child psychologist, which suggested he had Asperger's Syndrome. At the time, I had never heard of this syndrome, but upon hours of research, I realized this diagnosis affects every male in my family.

The commonalities we share are also like what I have seen out of President Putin. Putin is highly intelligent, ahead of the game by years, successful in his own finances, quick tempered, and appears to lack empathy when looking on the outside. He is a rock on his throne, likely from his disorder and years of being molded by the KGB to be emotionless, which would be easier coming from someone with Asperger's Syndrome. In my own observations, Putin's actions are very predictable and understandable, without giving positive praise to his invasion.

Adolf Hitler will forever go down in history as evil incarnate by the mass murder of millions of European Jews. It is hard to look back at what happened in Europe in the '40s without thinking that Hitler had an intense mental condition. Motherjones.com states, "In 1943, the Office of Strategic Services, the CIA's World War II-era predecessor, commissioned Henry A. Murray of the Harvard Psychological Clinic to evaluate Hitler's personality based on remote observations." Murray concluded, "Hitler was an insecure, impotent, masochistic, and suicidal neurotic narcissist who saw himself as the destroyer of an antiquated Hebraic Christian superego." Murray later stated, "There is little disagreement among professional, or even among amateur, psychologists that Hitler's personality is an example of the counteractive type, a type that is marked by intense and stubborn efforts to overcome early disabilities, weaknesses and humiliations (wounds to self-esteem), and sometimes also by efforts to revenge injuries and insults to pride." In short, Hitler had a troubled childhood where he was likely bullied for being inferior. He then bought into the German Empire under Emperor Kaiser Wilhelm while serving in the German military. When the empire fell in WWI, Hitler became enraged, as he likely became reminiscent of his days feeling helpless as a child while being bullied. Hitler then became engulfed into recreating Germany in his own image.

Hitler also had issues sexually. Murray found, "Sexually he is a full-fledged masochist...Hitler's long-concealed secret heterosexual fantasy has been exposed by the systemic analysis and correlation of the three thousand odd metaphors he usus in Mein Kampf..." and yet Hitler himself is impotent. He is unmarried, and his old acquaintances say that he is incapable of consummating the sexual act in a normal fashion. As we often wonder why Hitler's sexual desires are relevant, in fact they help fully give a rounded view of what the man was thinking in a complex way instead of just merely stating he is a psychopath.

His narcissism made him too loyal to himself while being too loyal to his overall objectives, which led to his eventual suicide. If we take away Hitler's undeniable desire to murder every Jew on the planet, we can see the intelligent design of technological advancements and research that he achieved during his reign. In fact, most of our modern technology derived from ideas of the 194's Nazis. In some ways, it is these types of thinking people that advance our existence. I would put Elon Musk in that same category; however, what separates man from innovative hero to dictator is the individual's ability to not cross that mental line of absolute control, which generally leads to unempathetic death.

In 1961, the CIA published their own psychological assessment of Cuban Dictator Fidel Castro. Their findings read as follow, "Fidel Castro is not crazy, but he is so highly neurotic and unstable a personality as to be quite vulnerable to certain kinds of psychological pressure. The outstanding neurotic elements in his personality are his hunger for power and his need for the recognition and adulation of the masses…" I find this statement to make a lot of sense, as Castro always appeared to be one click away from losing his mind yet kept a slight teeter inside the realm of logic. I believe that since his reign in Cuba lasted, if it did, until his death, he had a very tight control over his people and military. If fact, it was so tight that our own intelligence agencies could not infiltrate his inner circle. Even after the Bay of Pigs, Castro remained unconquered, which as Cuba's close proximity to the US was an impressive feat.

The CIA further stated, "Castro has a constant need to rebel, to find an adversary, and to extend his personal power by overthrowing existing authority. Whenever his self-concept is slightly disrupted by criticism, he becomes so emotionally unstable as to lose to some degree his contact with reality… Castro's egoism is his Achilles heel." I have mixed feelings about the CIA's excerpt of Castro, his egoism was not his Achilles heel. The fact that the dictator was never conquered despite all the efforts to do so shows that Castro's strategy within his own borders was in fact successful through a dictator's eyes. To normal-thinking people, a violent ego is a horrendous thing to have, which can self-sabotage the agenda by allowing unrealistic thought patterns mask what is meant to be in effect.

For decades, Libya has been a pain in the side of almost every non-Muslim nation on the planet. Their dictator, Moammar Qaddafi, is among one of the worst human beings that has ever lived. In Bob Woodward's book, *Veil*, he quoted the CIA's assessment of Qaddafi by stating; "Despite popular belief to the contrary, Qaddafi is not psychotic, and for the most part is in contact with reality… Qaddafi is judged to suffer from a severe personality disturbance- a borderline personality disorder… Under severe stress, his is subject to bizarre behavior when his judgment may be faulty." The CIA, in a way, downplayed Qaddafi's evil mindset by stating he only has a borderline personality disorder. If that diagnosis held true, it is not can of beans. This man can go down several highly destructive paths within his own brain and, along with his military power, can in fact be the hand of as many deaths as he would like, which often occurred during his reign. The CIA even went on to state that Qaddafi's behavior looks like "an approaching or actual midlife crisis." A midlife crisis? That agent is either a tyrant or underqualified to give a professional assessment on behalf of the CIA.

It is safe to say that we are not that far away from the effect Saddam Hussein had on the Middle East. During the first Gulf War in 1991, Hussein attempted to invade Kuwait, which ended in President George HW Bush giving the full weight of the American Military powerhouse to destroy Iraq in around a hundred hours. That war is the last modern war that the US has been great in. General Norman Schwartzkopf brilliantly and quickly developed the plan to neutralize the Middle East with perfection. It was the last time the US would prove we are in fact the biggest dog on the block.

In 1990, Jerrold Post, the founder of the CIA's now-defunct Center for the Analysis of Personality and Political Behavior, presented a comprehensive political psychology profile of Saddam to the House Armed Services Committee. Post's report, in my opinion, hit the nail on the head. Post stated,

The labels madman of the Middle East and megalomaniac are often affixed to Saddam, but in fact there is no evidence that he is suffering from a psychotic disorder. Saddam's pursuit of power for himself and Iraq is boundless. In fact, in his mind, the destiny of Saddam and Iraq are one and indistinguishable… In pursuit of his messianic dreams, there is no evidence he is constrained by conscience; his only loyalty is to Saddam Hussein. In pursuing his goals, Saddam uses aggression instrumentally. He uses whatever force is necessary, and will, if he deems it expedient, go to extremes of violence, including the use of weapons of mass destruction… While Hussein is not psychotic, he has a strong paranoid orientation… Saddam has no wish to be a martyr, and survival is his number one priority. A self-proclaimed revolutionary pragmatist, he does not wish a conflict in which Iraq will be grievously damaged and his stature as leader be destroyed… Saddam will not go down to the last flaming bunker if he has a way out, but he can be extremely dangerous and will stop at nothing if her is backed into a corner.

I think Post had a good handle on Hussein; however, as the future from his article unfolded, we now know, Hussein did in fact go down to the last bunker, literally. We also know that after watching one of his hearings in the US, he was very convicted in his hate for the US. Post was right in the sense that Hussein only believed in Hussein. His statements in court proved that to be true. At the end of the day, Hussein was just another power-hungry dictator that was paranoid of everyone.

It is a wonder that some of these dictators made it to power without a single day of political ambition. Most were not elected to anything; instead, they used their military rank and power to simply bully anyone in the way, which in turn allowed them to lead the country. This kind of rule is called a stratocracy. In the US, the likelihood of this being the case is slim to none. Our two-party system has too much power over our military leaders, which are extremely obedient despite the growing number of military politicians among the ranks.

It appears that most of the world's past and present dictatorship-type countries have military-style leadership. As there are several different ways to become a dictator, the end doesn't seem to change. In the world today, there are fifty-two countries that have a dictator for a leader, while most are in Asia. The one thing that nearly all of these countries have in common is they are often considered third-world nations. Most are poor and struggle to fund anything other than war with whomever resists them. The list is very clear: Afghanistan, Algeria, Angola, Azerbaijan, Bahrain, Bangladesh, Belarus, Brunei Burundi, Cambodia, Cameroon, Central African Republic, Chad, China, Congo x2, Cuba, Djibouti, Egypt, Equatorial Guinea, Eritrea, Ethiopia, Gabon, Iran, Iraq, Kazakhstan, Laos, Libya, Myanmar, Nicaragua, North Korea, Oman, Qatar, Russia, Rwanda, Saudi Arabia, Somalia, South Sudan, Sudan, Swaziland, Syria, Tajikistan, Tibet, Turkey, Turkmenistan, Uganda, UAE, Uzbekistan, Venezuela, Vietnam, Western Sahara, and Yemen. Every single one of these nations is fighting to keep their economy afloat. Some are a little better off than most; however, by next year I predict, 20 percent of these nations will have changed leadership.

Dictatorship is a dangerous game that attracts many enemies, which in turn keeps the leaders locked down in their palaces in fear of assassination. It is astounding that the great democracy of the United States of America would have politicians that would support any of the aforementioned nations. We should not be modeling our nation after these failures.

One very big mistake that I believe all these dictators make is censorship. Censoring your people will allow for unrest as we are social beings and when leadership stops listening to the people, the people will find other ways to be heard. In most of the current socialist countries, there are two factions: the regime/military presence and the resistance. Having oppressed people causes uprisings from resistance groups, which will generally make the whole nation a war zone with many unnecessary deaths.

President Biden, I feel, is going to feel the wrath of this historically bad decision that most dictators make. In late April of 2022, Biden appointed known, radical left, Nina Jankowicz as executive director of his newly minted Disinformation Governance Board. The White House won't directly admit it, but the creation of this new government department is a direct result of Elon Musk buying and privatizing Twitter in mid-April. It is very concerning that as soon as socialist Democrats loose total control of the information riddled social media world due to a major company buyout, they create a government branch to combat it.

This agency is going to make or break Elon Musk and will also make or break the Democrats for the upcoming elections as it will reveal their true colors to even their voting base that even White House propagandist, Jen Psaki can't spin. My prediction is, Nina Jankowicz will spend a lot of time micromanaging Twitter users, along with Trump's Truth Social, while leaving Facebook and other left leaning Constitution violators alone. Government regulation of free speech is a violation of the US Constitution in itself. Every American on this planet should be screaming at the top of their lungs to dismantle this department of our government. Musk is clearly the most intelligent individual on the planet, and I believe that when push comes to shove, the government is going to try to label everything on twitter misinformation like they claimed when the Hunter Biden laptop story came out, although we later found out the information to be very true. Musk is going to sue this agency a lot, however, the Biden intention is to put some time in-between the event reveal on social media and when the DOJ proves it true. Biden has been able to avoid heavy damage this way while watering down the truth later to avoid a negative public effect. Most people will take the government at face value, so when the White House states something is not true, the masses generally take that as true.

If Biden is outfoxed by Musk, which he certainly will, we will see an aggressive maneuver of some sorts to shut Twitter down. After the First Amendment is destroyed by the hands of the US Government, the nation will react as the veil will be lifted. At the end of the day, the government needs us, we don't need them.

As a dictator, I don't feel the need to suppress the people from speaking their truths. If they are not conspiring to assassinate me as the leader of the country or threaten bodily harm against anyone else, say what you want. Everyone is entitled to have a high functioning brain in my regime. If I allow for the people to keep their creative dignity, they will be less likely to uprise against me in the future. After all, we are forever students in this world, and I will never stop learning how to be a better human to my people. Censorship is a grave mistake that Biden is making that will have dire repercussions in the future.

Censorship is not a necessary tool to control the masses. It is a desperate measure to silence ordinary people that the government cannot control with their policies. If government policies are solid and understood by the people, there would be no need to silence anyone. Biden feels the need to do this because his policies are so far left that even the moderate Democrats have turned their backs on him. If US leadership would stand for most of the country, there would be no need for censorship.

Having an inadequate president that is either too incompetent or too controlled has taken its toll on everyday Americans. If government officials would just be honest with their constituents rather than treat us like we are naïve, there would be more progress to further advance our way of live to leave countries like China and Russia in the dust. The Biden way has weakened our country as did the full spectrum of Trump's way. The difference between the two is Biden is controlled by individuals with too radical of an agenda, where Trump had his heart in the right spot, but his delivery lacked sincerity. Therefore, I truly believe Trump's leadership was more effective on all fronts. Anyone that doesn't think America should be first probably needs to find a new country. In my America, I would create a moderation system among some of the most down-the-middle individuals the country has to offer. These chosen few would be responsible for looking at both sides of the spectrum in order to help me make a moderated decision from my advisors. At the end of the day, I would do what I think is right for my country and my people. Committees of experts that have no special interests are how you get major issues does.

When we summarize what socialist, communist dictatorship has meant to us now, along with in the past and future, we can clearly understand that if this country wants to head in that direction, we should be modeling ourselves on what has been successful instead of the historically failed methods of Marx, Lenin, Stalin, and Hitler. Americans also need to take control of every inch of the country that has been polluted by all of the back-door lies being told to us by spineless cowards. My country will be built on strength, pride, and wisdom from the very people that are the building blocks of this nation, Americans.

Take a good long look at yourself in the mirror, American. Are you going to conform to failure brought forth by leftist, masked cowards, or will you stand with me, sword of our ancestors from all over the world in hand, to bring pride and hope back to the greatest nation known to man?

www.ingramcontent.com/pod-product-compliance
Lightning Source LLC
Chambersburg PA
CBHW050917260726
48660CB00001B/246